# Million Dollar Mommy
## Six Secrets

Nancy Pollard, L.C.S.W & Laura Tanner

Bloomington, IN  Milton Keynes, UK

authorHOUSE

*AuthorHouse*™
*1663 Liberty Drive, Suite 200*
*Bloomington, IN 47403*
*www.authorhouse.com*
*Phone: 1-800-839-8640*

*AuthorHouse*™ *UK Ltd.*
*500 Avebury Boulevard*
*Central Milton Keynes, MK9 2BE*
*www.authorhouse.co.uk*
*Phone: 08001974150*

*First published by AuthorHouse 2/23/2006*

*ISBN: 1-4259-1731-3 (e)*
*ISBN: 1-4259-1730-5 (sc)*
*ISBN: 1-4259-1729-1 (dj)*

*Library of Congress Control Number: 2006901202*

*Printed in the United States of America*
*Bloomington, Indiana*

*This book is printed on acid-free paper.*

# Dedication

**To the Dads who made us Moms and**
**The Cherished Children born**


**To All Mothers**
**Before us,**
**With us &**
**After us**

# We would like to acknowledge:

Meg Snyder for her relentless and incredible editing talents, Ryan Nicholas for his perseverance in getting the art work just right, Kelly Ardern Boyd for her graphic and copy design talents, and Getty Pollard for his willingness to review and critique with his impeccable eye whatever was sent his way. Mary McPherson for loving the book from start to finish and Bonny Royce whom reminded us to give the book more love. Jane Caspe who believes in this project and me. Thank you all so much.

Chuck Gates, Andy Cier, Jim Stith, and Peg Bodell for their expertise and valued opinions. All of our wonderful Mom participants who had no time and found the time to complete the survey for this project. We thank our friends, families and colleagues for their support and encouragement to see this project through to fruition.

The authors acknowledge one another in their own mutual admiration society and the synergy that made Million Dollar Mommy, Six Secrets a reality. Without the other, the book would have remained only an idea.

# Contents

# ~ 1 ~

# Introduction

My body ached. I was literally being sucked dry. After nursing, the second time that night, I collapsed into bed and immediately fell into a deep sleep and vivid dream. I am driving my car along a long stretch of road. Suddenly, and for a reason I cannot remember, my car swerves off of the road and lands upside down in a creek. My body is pinned in the car but somehow I manage to get my son out. We are fully submerged underwater but my arms hold him above the waterline. I can see from my underwater position that he is going to be fine, but I know that I am going to drown. The last thing I remember thinking in my dream is at least he is going to live.

My journey into motherhood feels much like my dream. It is not a big stretch to see how the dream was my subconscious interpretation of how it felt to be totally responsible for another human being, and how I had to sacrifice my own life to make sure that he lived; or so I thought especially those first six weeks of motherhood.

This story is a common one. The journey into motherhood is full of unexpected surprises. How much you love your children, how amazing they are, how intelligent they are, what they give you, and how much they take. For some, it isn't until about the sixth week of motherhood that it dawns on them that motherhood wasn't about having a life like it was before with the addition of an extra body. Motherhood is all consuming and life changing to the extent that one can rarely anticipate. This is particularly true for women that have their children later in life and have had a successful career.

Many mothers' stories tell of tales of being emotionally hijacked by motherhood. Repeatedly women report shock and surprise at the dramatic impact motherhood has on them. They even express anger at their naiveté. Over and over again it is expressed, ' I should have been elated that I was a mother, but I actually feel like the whole experience had been misrepresented to me.' Most career women truly have every intention of continuing on their career path. They had no idea that they would no longer be an important consultant, a valued account executive, or powerful vice president continuing the promising career that they had been engaged in for the prior decade. For many of the women life as they knew it was literally over; right down to the wardrobe closet, where silk blouses and linen business suits collected dust and were replaced with sweats, workout clothes and t-shirts that could be laundered over and over again. One such woman literally emptied the professional wardrobe from her closet with the exception of one black dress, one sundress and one woolen skirt and top.

There seems to be an expectation in our society about what a "successful" woman should be able to accomplish. You often hear things like, 'she had a baby and didn't miss a beat' or, 'she does it all-works, takes care of the baby, and maintains the household.' Is it really ideal to do it all? Do CEO's do it all? Do highly successful people ever do it all, all by themselves? Is any great leader truly great all by him- or herself? Trying to do it all downplays and ignores the importance of a woman taking care of herself. For a woman who has made the decision to quit or downsize her career responsibilities, she can easily feel like she's not as good as that "ideal" woman who "does it all." If you can "do it all," more power to you. If you choose not to, maybe you are more honest, realistic or possibly even smarter. Maybe you have given yourself permission to do it all…just not all of it at the same time.

According to Kathy Kolbe in her latest book, "Pure Instinct, the M.O. of High Performance People and Teams," she discusses the power of teamwork at great length. Ms. Kolbe maintains that an organization enjoys the greatest competitive advantage when it builds teams that have a synergistic mix of striving instincts. Is it possible to consider that a mom and a dad comprise such a team? Wouldn't parents and child alike thrive in a similar set-up? Perhaps doing it all yourself is not necessarily a good or wise thing.

If your children are older and not yet teenagers, you have already probably adjusted to motherhood, found motherhood more enjoyable and rewarding than you did when your children were newborns, and forgotten the late night feedings, the sleep deprivation, the diaper changing, and the throw-up on your shirt…for the third time. As your children get older, these early motherhood episodes get drowned out with the thrill of the first step, the first tooth, the first Ma-Ma, Da-Da, the first day of school, first soccer game, and first project science fair. For you mothers with older children who decided to stay at home or work part-time while your children lived through the baby and toddler stages, give yourself a big pat on the back. If it is time for you to jump back into society's workforce, leaving your own workplace of the home, feel proud of a job well done.

Remember, you did the best you could with who you were at the time. If you could have made any other choices, you would have. You do not have to feel a sense of loss from being out of the workforce. If you were raising babies, you know that it is like no other job in the world. You know the challenges, the frustrations and the accomplishments you made. Don't feel that you need to apologize for your decisions. You did what was right for you and your children, and you should feel extremely proud of the job you have done. And while seasoned mothers can find solace and empowerment from Million Dollar Mommy, the book is designed to target 25-40 year old career minded women before they have children, and particularly the new Moms with children under 5.

If you are a new mother, how often do you sneak away in the stillness of the night or the privacy of your own closet or bathroom sobbing your heart out from exhaustion?  How frequently do you rock your little precious one, closing your eyes and daring to not speak aloud what you are thinking because it sounds so horrible?  How is it that you feel so terribly helpless and hopeless at what you have gotten yourself into?  Why didn't anyone tell you that this would be the hardest job you have ever done?  No seriously. Honestly.  Who told you that you could lose your self-esteem and your self worth?  Who told you that pumping breast milk could make you feel like a cow in a barn, that life could literally be sucked out of you?  How could the waves of emotions continue night after night and day after day, the highs and the lows all at once within minutes of each other?

You are not alone is these overwhelming feelings.  And probably every generation of mothers producing children has experienced the rough times smacked in the face with incredibly precious moments.  For the career and professional woman, your journey is magnified ten times over with unexpected choices and consequences.

*The day was long and I was tired.  From dawn until dusk I heard, 'tie my shoes....gimme a drink....I'm hungry...! They were nitpicking demands, little aggravations, one too many cups of milk spilled, insignificant occurrences that peck away at patience.  It was a day of constant attention and confusion, answering needs and meeting requests.  Bedtime for my three-year-old was a time I had been silently looking forward to all day long.  As the clock struck eight, the magic hour arrived, off to bed we trooped.  I secretly prayed to myself that tonight it would be a simple matter, no fusses, no crying, just sleep.  After our usual bedtime ritual of potty, drink, and prayers, tonight one more request was asked of me.  "Sing 'Sunshine' to me Mommy," my three- year old son said.  SING! I thought to myself.  You want me to sing! I'll shout.  I'll yell.  How can I sing when my patience is worn thin, dinner is still to be served, homework with your older brother, dishes to do! How can I control myself to sing a gentle loving lullaby!*

*Guilt, a common mothering feeling, came over me.  Was it his fault he had an older brother who had homework?  Was it his fault Dad had gotten home late and was hungry?  Was it his fault I was not Supermom, who never runs out of patience and time?*

*"Ok," I agreed. - "I'll sing one song, but that is it. No more!" He blinked gratefully at me, melting a bit of my heart, innocence staring me in the face.  Taking a deep breath, I began to sing, "Sunshine on my shoulders*

*makes me happy...sunshine on the water looks so lovely... sunshine almost always makes me high..." The melody was soothing. As I sang to him in the stillness and intimacy of the moment, my voice was beautiful ...to him. My sourness was quickly sweetened. He patted my face. He is three, this son of mine and already a master of loving. He cuddled in the covers and looked at me. "I love you Mommy," he whispered sleepily, relaxed and at peace. In one fell swoop, a day of demands and trials was erased. "I love you too, sweetness," I answered. This is a silent gift of parenting. It happens and it helps.*

There are many tender moments that melt your heart and give you the courage to face another day. But what about the many nights that you are startled awake one more time with a crying child? And adding insult to injury, somehow magically your spouse can sleep through. This is an age-long comment from women of multiple generations. "He sleeps right through the baby wailing!" If it's of any consolation, there is a scientific reason behind this fact, according to Helen Fisher's research in her book titled *The First Sex The Natural Talents of Women and How They are Changing the World* (The First Sex):

"Women on average...have superior hearing. Who hears the faucet dripping as husband and wife drift off to sleep? The woman. Why? The answer lies in deep history. An ancestral woman needed superb hearing... on the plains of ancient Africa, women listened to their infants, listened to the wind and rain, listened for snakes and cats and rapacious birds, then listened to their own hearts to save their young."

You now know that with your mother instincts, you will never be able to be deaf again; unless you discover that it's another person's child, and then you only experience relief that it is not your own. It is normal to be overwhelmed, sleep deprived, really down and then really up all within minutes.

It is part of motherhood. You are not alone. Every mother has and will have her own unspoken nightmare of moments. Many educated mothers, highly sophisticated once career-oriented, goal driven, Type "A" executives can be reduced to feelings of Cinderella, dish washing, floor mopping servitude.

This is not a "woe is me" book. This is a book that says it is damn tough as well as the most phenomenal experience of your life. This book may help you to figure out why you got into this mess in the first place and find a way to be more comfortable and secure in your decision to be a Mom. Find peace in your choice whether it's to be a Stay-at-Home Mom, Part- or full-time career Mom, and be able to truly reap the rewards in spite of the stress that being a mother can bring. There are some tricks of the trade that will help both you and your spouse succeed and maintain excellent mental and emotional health and well-being as you journey through the first few years of motherhood. This book will also help open your eyes to the fact that the overwhelmed and sucked-dry feelings can and should be balanced by a sense of pride and accomplishment of tackling the tough and important job of parenting – a job which has no equal.

The authors, Nancy Pollard, LCSW, Certified Empowerment Coach, and Laura Tanner, a career woman, now full time stay at home Mom, planted the seed of this book at the end of one of their coaching sessions. Together they tripped over the language of being emotionally hijacked by motherhood; and both knew the moment the words were spoken, a book was in the making. For the next year, they collaborated on what was happening to Laura, and reflected what had happened to Nancy almost a generation ago.

Colleagues and friends started offering input and with that a survey was constructed and sent out to approximately 40 mothers that met the age requirements of being between 25 and 40 that had children under the age(s) of five. The more Nancy and Laura talked about the book, the more encouraged they were to move forward on the idea and concept.

Thus, a MILLION DOLLAR MOMMY, Six Secrets was born.

# ~ 2 ~

# Emotionally Hijacked by Motherhood

$\mathcal{A}$n Emotional Hijacking is what happens to Moms. More specifically, feeling depressed, exhausted, resentful, guilty, worried, anxious, incompetent, alone, and generally not good enough, are all indications that you've been emotionally hijacked.

A definition of an emotional hijacking is a physiological response in a person's brain based on emotions that keeps them from thinking clearly. So it would stand to reason that new mothers are prime candidates for emotional hijacking, more so than other adults simply because they are undergoing a variety of abnormal physiological conditions, particularly sleep deprivation and hormonal changes.

*I felt like I was floundering during my child's first year and in the whole parenting picture, alone. I felt alone being the mother. I was working part time in my career. My life felt surreal. I was dog-tired all of the time and mostly felt like I was just going through the motions. My days were a blur of feeding, clothing, bathing my child, writing reports in a daze, and collapsing into sleep at the end of the day, only to wake up several times a night to feed my child. I was being sucked dry in every aspect of my life. Everything was taking from me and I was very negligent about replenishing me.*

*Yeah, yeah, I know, I've read all the books about how important it is to make time for me, but time was the very item that seemed to be lacking. In addition, I did not possess the tools in my toolbox to make sure that I did take care of me. Instead, the resentment began to build. Everyone and everything began to look threatening to the very fragile amount of self that I had left. I didn't want to go where the experience was taking me, and yet we deliberately got pregnant again. Time was ticking, and we wanted to have two children. I guess I figured we'd work it out later.*

Does this story sound familiar? It may be illogical, you may not want to go where the experience is taking you, but you do it anyway. How many of you forgot to take care of yourself as a new Mom? How many of you, scheduled time-outs, pedicures, massages, lunch with an old girlfriend, help from a nanny, grandparent or aunt? As a woman, who by nature is good at giving, giving, giving, being there for anyone and everyone, of course you are going to turn up as the quintessential caregiver to your newborn. It is in your genes, your wiring, and your socialization. The story goes on.

*I began to blame my helpless, victimized feelings on hormones and my husband. I felt under-appreciated and over-taxed and began to feel like it was his fault. After all, I hadn't become a parent by myself, but it seemed to me that all of the parental obligations fell squarely on my shoulders, and frankly, my back was beginning to hurt.*

Women are good at being martyrs on the home front, taking on the world single-handedly. Mothers are good at not asking for help, being too proud, wanting to be "supermom", or too guilty to admit that they are totally overwhelmed and too emotionally hijacked to think straight.

*I had several conversations with my husband trying to point out the injustice of the arrangement. I was working outside of the home, pregnant, and doing everything for our child and maintaining the house. The way I saw it he was off doing whatever it was that he did...getting haircuts, playing 18 holes of golf, and having drinks with his friends. I was home, at times covered in spit-up, feeling chained to my child and the house and getting fatter by the minute.*

Sometimes you're simply too exhausted to fight with your husband. You try to beg, barter and explain how tired you are, how you still love him, but just have no more to give. You finally shut down, do the whole parenting gig alone, never bother him with the babies, and become increasingly resentful. Your resentment keeps you distant, cold, and uninterested in your husband whose life does not seem to have changed at all, and who has become just another need to be met.

*Regardless of the vivid examples and finger waving, my husband just did not seem to get it! His comment was, "well, you can go out whenever you want; you just need to schedule it with me." The outrage! He never bothered to schedule things with me. And so things went on, the pregnancy and delivery of my second child, were enough to knock the wind out of my sail. After the second 6-week milestone, I was a physical and mental wreck. It was enough to send the sanest person over the edge, not that I am claiming sanity.*

Often in overwhelm, we are not thinking straight. The above scenario clearly speaks of depression. Unquestionably every single new mother goes through some sort of depression at some point. According to the survey results, 80% of our mothers responded that they have suffered from symptoms of depression. The clinical definition of depression is helplessness and hopelessness. Depression could also be called depletion. Mothers, especially new ones, get depleted on probably every level, physically, mentally, and emotionally. As the depletion continues, an emotional hijacking results.

# ~ 3 ~

## The Mighty Media and Role Models

What is wrong with the picture that new mothers have painted for themselves? More importantly why do they let this happen?

There are many reasons that a new mother may become emotionally hijacked, not the least of which are the historical and social views of mothers and motherhood. There seems to be an unspoken model in modern day consciousness that a woman should fit once she becomes a mother. June Cleaver comes to mind. Remember her? The *Leave it to Beaver* Mom? Do you know any women that fit this model? In an article written by Ann Hulbert titled, *The Real Myth of Motherhood,* women have been writing about and lamenting this mother stereotype for nearly three decades now. Time Magazine's March 14, 1977 edition featured a cover story called "The New Housewife Blues," and a portion of the article states that, "...the American housewife is suffering from a fundamental uncertainty about what a housewife is or should be." Unfortunately for today's mother, almost thirty years later, the question still has yet to be answered satisfactorily.

According to the same March 14, 1977 Time Magazine Article, "At best, the rearing of children is a fascinating and rewarding occupation. But at worst, the mopping up of spilled food and the changing of diapers are menial labor of the lowest sort, dirty, boring, wearying and endless. The housewife gets no salary, no promotions, no titles, and no formal evidence that the maintenance of family life is, as Jimmy Carter said in his Inaugural Address, 'the basis of our society.'"

It seems that despite all the information written about mothers and motherhood in our society, the feelings of frustration, loneliness, depression, and worthlessness still haunt generation after generation of mothers. Maybe this is just an American social "challenge". Interestingly, one Latin American woman, 35ish, with two babies under the age of 4 is an awesome Mom. She takes her role very seriously and is proud of what she does. Her husband possibly chose her for her warm familial open-heartedness. Her mother was married to her father at age 16. They are still together more than 40 years later. Her mother was a mother, always a mother, and is still a mother, as is her grandmother. This is a prime example of how different cultures and different values produce different expectations. This woman also did not walk away from a six-figure income. She is a college graduate and very talented, but when she decided to have children, there was nothing more to say. She would stay at home and raise them-- end of conversation.

Why is it that we as American women and mothers still revert back to the ideology of the 1950's and 1960's to try to model perfect mother behavior? Perhaps it's because that in spite of the fact that many women have written about the hardships of motherhood, it is not a topic that many women explore if they have not yet become mothers. Further, when a woman makes the transition from career person to mother, no matter how many books she's read, friends she's surveyed or decisions she's made about how she going to parent, she can feel blindsided.

The truth is, motherhood has changed tremendously over the past 60 years. Female role models have changed every decade, but there is a definite lack of current mother role models. The 1940's and 1950's the media introduced the perfect mother in the sitcom 'Ozzie and Harriet'. Women then, knew what was to be expected of them. Get married and have children. The term 'stay-at-home Mom' would have been an oxymoron. Of course they stayed home with their children; if they didn't it could have been viewed as low class and looked down upon.

In the 1960's women liberation came along and began to plant the seeds that would give women the choice, the power, the equality to work outside of the home. It appears however, that it was easier when (God forbid!) Women did women's work and Men did men's work. You know the hunter and the gatherer, chop wood and carry water. Men knew who they were and whom they were supposed to be and women knew who they were and what role they were to fill. Yes, barefoot and pregnant seems a tidy definition. The only problem is that life keeps changing; new technology creates totally different lifestyles. My grandmother could hang out her wash and visit with her neighbor discussing when the tomatoes in the garden would be ripe and they could spend the day canning, while all the little children tugged at their apron strings and played with salt water and flour play dough. In hindsight, it looks pretty easy.

According to information presented in a November 1993 issue of _Working Woman_, we had in the 1960's our first super model, Twiggy, '...A boy. A doll with painted lashes.' The 70's brought us Mary Tyler Moore, an independent woman developing authority. Yes, Mary Richards did call her boss Mr. Grant, while he called her Mary. And yes, as a circa-'70's woman surrounded by men on the job, she did experience an occasional burst of insecurity. Still she didn't need a man to be happy, and she showed that women really were going to make it in the workplace after all.

Then there was Faye Dunaway as the ruthless executive who demonstrated what supposedly happens to a woman who tries to play corporate games like a man. Her lust for control ultimately made her emotionally sterile, and because she loved power more than she loved anything-even love- she wound up with neither.

In the 1980's Joan Collins played Alexis Carrington, the ultimate example of the woman-who –rhymes-with-rich personifying the era, and out clawing everyone else on Dynasty. The 1990's brought us Hillary Rodham Clinton who has clearly changed the job title from First Lady to First Woman and probably paved the way for the first woman President. None of these women show us how to be stay-at- home Moms, or how to be fulfilled as a mother or how to take motherhood as a serious profession or how to balance career and family. Isn't it true in today's media that there are no positive Mom role models? Even in the current situation comedy *Desperate Housewives*, the focus is not on the trial and tribulations of motherhood.

With the onslaught of information available in the world, and the lack of decent role models, it's no wonder that mothers can easily feel inferior about the choices that they have made, and it's worthy of note that guilt and competitiveness play a central role. There's a parenting book on just about anything you can dream up. You could be an "attachment" style parent, a "breast-feeder" a "bottle feeder" a "cry-it-out" parent…you name it, and there's a name for it. And while there is a tendency in our culture to attach labels to parenting styles and philosophies, there's nothing about a label that makes anyone feel good. Aerial Gore's book, *The Hip Mama's Survival Guide,* contains a chapter called "Labels that Make You Feel Bad" to emphasize some of the ways that our culture brands mothers by what they do or don't do. Unfortunately, with all of the labels out there, some people have a tendency to judge mothers, and mothers have a tendency to judge themselves using other people as their yardsticks. Don't do it, or at least try not to. Remember, it's difficult to see movie star Moms return to their former stick-thin selves within hours of delivery. It makes most mothers feel bad because they still have some (or even most) of their baby weight around for many weeks or months after giving birth. But how many of you have several nannies and personal trainers at your disposal 24-hours a day?

*For some reason it feels like a personal failure on my part when I hear of the successes of others. I know that I wouldn't trade places with anyone that I know, but still I feel like I'm short on parenting or life skills somehow when I hear that someone walked out of the hospital in their pre-pregnancy jeans, or taught their child to read at age 2, or has a child that will only eat organic foods (and a good variety at that). My experience is that it took many, many months to return to my pre-pregnancy size, my toddlers don't read to me but love to have books read to them, and will only eat a handful of things, most of which could not be found in organic stores. Why is it then, that I can have happy, healthy children (they are rarely sick, are growing normally, and are well adjusted) and still feel like I'm doing something wrong? It's guilt, I know, and I need to get over it.*

The net result of the constant need to compare yourself to others is guilt. Have you met a Mom who is guilt-free? Shouldn't you all be?

Guilt is but one of the many emotional burdens that new mothers face. There is also pride. Parental pride is a powerful beast. The minute one becomes a Mom it is impossible to not notice how others are parenting. It is also a breeding ground for judgment. 'I can't believe that so and so lets her baby sleep in the bed with them.... I can't believe that she is not breast feeding her baby....I can't believe that she leaves her child with a nanny all day. I can't believe that she lets her child stay up so late. I can't believe that she doesn't make her child take a time out. I can't believe that she is so hard on her son and so forgiving and coddling with her daughter...' There are also the instances of mothers comparing their children's activities. It seems that there's a value placed on getting your kids into the 'right' school, or on the 'right' sports team- a value by which your value as a parent is measured. For the most part, today's mothers are guilty of over-scheduling themselves via their children's activities, and then they feel guilty about not having enough quality time.

And these are only young mothers talking about other young mothers. There is also your mother or your mother-in-law telling you how to do it.

Unsolicited advice to anyone on anything is usually a bad idea, but particularly a bad idea to a new mom who is extremely emotionally vulnerable and sensitive. There are always the instant experts who have just read the latest child psychology books and research and declare to anyone that will listen, 'Absolutely DO NOT let your child sleep on his stomach. DO NOT..., DO NOT..., blah, blah, blah...'

Every generation has its wisdom on child rearing. On cold winter nights a generation ago, the mandate of no blankets in the crib would have been scoffed at. This was the generation that grew up without seatbelts, car seats, and alcohol and wine being okay while pregnant. Somehow the children of that generation made it to adulthood, despite sleeping on their tummies with their favorite blankie. Earth Mothers of the 70's did not use anything artificial - no processed foods, no Gerber canned dinners, no pampers. Cloth diapers hung out on the line to dry in fresh air, and of course, breast-fed straight to the sippy cup! Women who are now in their 80's considered it to be low class to breast feed. Only the poor did that. Not only is there a plethora of advice for parents of each generation, there is also a surplus of judgment, criticism and guilt. Often one generation contradicts the next.

More fodder for guilt is the legal issues that surround our parenting styles today. Sometimes the legal issues are used as a means of measuring your worth as a parent or judging others. If you see a parent with their children in a car without having the proper seats and/or restraining devices, you pass judgment. Certainly our society has created a whole plethora of things that you must do now because of litigation, that were simply not issues in the 1970's. Car seats, a crib bar spacing, walkers, and safety recalls are all the results of tragedies or accidents that led to legislation. Which, in turn, have led to yet another yardstick used by moms to compare their own competence in light of other parents.

Guilt, judgment, comparison and competition can eat away at you and make you feel like a bad parent. You feel like you are failing your kids if they are not checked into the best preschool, if you can't afford the most fashionable wardrobe, if you don't expose them to every classical composer by age 2, and a myriad of other things. Parents living in this millennium have more awareness of not gender stereotyping their children by giving them options of all sorts. This means in the simplest of examples, offering little boys dolls and little girls Tonka trucks. Women's lib can be credited for raising our awareness of equality and not stereotyping. This is such a good conceptual idea. It may or may not work. Today, with very progressive, open-minded, and educated parents, little girls can still be seen choosing the baby stroller, pretending to be a mommy and pulling up their shirts to nurse their pretend babies. Little boys can still be found throwing anything they can get away with throwing, climbing whatever they can climb and gravitating toward tools and toolboxes. Keep offering dolls to little boys and trucks to little girls. Try it. It is a good idea. And then watch, the child will let you know. The research has shown that there are truly gender-neutral toys. Whew! Good old Teddy still wins the hearts of both boys and girls.

Notwithstanding all of the information, stereotypes, and guilt, here's what you need to know: nothing makes you a bad parent...other than physical, emotional, mental abuse or neglect. As long as you're not doing any of those things, chances are, your children will turn out okay. Give yourself a break. You are doing the best you can with where you are at the moment. And if you are screwing up, your kids will let you know. They will act out, misbehave, cry a lot and be miserable to be around. The best monitor and judge of your parenting style is a happy, secure child.

So now that you're a Mom, who is your role model? Anyone you care to emulate? It doesn't fit to be your Mom or your Grandmother for that matter. Times have changed too drastically. Is it possible, that you young mothers between the ages of 25 and 40 are creating the mother role models of the future? What will you be modeling to your sons and daughters as they grow up in your household? Are you a doormat? A chauffeur? A cook? A bottle washer? Do you have a 'life' outside of mothering? And if so, what does it look like? Are you happy? Are you fulfilled? Are you proud of and content with your nest of chicks? Is your husband proud of you? Is he your best friend and loudest supporter, heralding your daily accomplishments with vim and vigor? What if it is up to you to create your own role models? Your generation is quite capable of creating whatever you want. Since the outside world provides only sparse and sporadic empowering Mom role models to emulate, perhaps this project falls into your lap. YOU. You, young mothers are creating the next role models for Stay-at-Home Moms, Part-time and Full-time Career Moms. What do you want it to look like? How can you command respect and elevate your role to the special and honored position it deserves?

Don't forget to include your spouse's role when you forge your model. Dads can be very instrumental is teaching children about Moms in general. Dads by their actions more so than their words can shout the message loud and clear about the importance of Mom and how she is the Saint of the Household, the Captain of the Mother Ship, and someone to be revered and honored. Dad can say to Mom after dinner...each dinner, actually... 'Wow, that was great, thanks for preparing a great meal, I loved it and I love you. It is so wonderful to have someone at home that has the time and the willingness to feed our family. Do you realize, Jack and Jill, that Mommy had to go to the store, unpack the groceries, put them away, find a recipe, cook it, set the table, serve the plates...just so we can have a nutritious meal?'

While the following sounds like a bit of a stretch, it is a true story.

*My Dad kissed my mother every single night after dinner and said, "Good dinner, Honey, thanks". I as well taught my sons that after dinner, and before they could leave the table, to say, 'may I be excused?' and then a kiss on the cheek for Mom as they took their plates to the sink. I witnessed my father idolizing my mother. He adored her, and her role as a wife and mother. So is it any wonder that I grew up valuing my role as a mother? It was easy for me. One, it is all that I ever wanted to be, and two, I was shown that it was the best role in the world!*

It is easy to believe that being a mom is the best job in the world if you are shown respect, value and daily appreciation. Unfortunately, most women have not had such positive parental role models. Some of the participants in our survey had negative mother role models. For example, one woman said that her mother saw her role as a mother as a sacrifice. What she sacrificed was her growth and career for raising her children. At least this is the participant's interpretation of her mother's opinion of being a full time Mom. This participant heard things like, 'Well, when you kids are gone, I'm going to do what *I* want to do!' Another participant's mother was reported to have sacrificed a successful career in the government. Her husband told her that he would not marry her if she did not stay home with the kids.

One participating Mom said that motherhood was taught to her to mean drudgery, sacrifice and a choice. What was the sacrifice? She interpreted it to mean her mother's sanity. This woman knew in spite of this that what she wanted to be was to be a Stay-at-Home Mom. And even though '… it is a struggle with having children close together in terms of lack of sleep, and having 'spirited' children, fortunately, I and especially my husband are able to be patient and loving…' She takes her job seriously. As does her husband. She sees it as her current profession and has the patience and wisdom to know that it is a time in her life that will one day be gone.

One of the Moms surveyed said that her mother was a psychologist and that is what she called herself. She herself saw herself keeping her career alive after children and in fact has done so. It is of importance to note that she and her husband pay $2500/month in childcare, $400/month in housecleaning and $150/month in gardening. She also has established vacation days and sick days, a perk of her career outside the home.

Another participant saw being able to stay home as a luxury. This comes from a mother who believes that she _has to_ work in order to live the life style that she and her husband want to live. In this day and age, creating a 'decent' lifestyle requires a certain number of dollars. Our standards of 'decent' have changed. Especially in the college-educated population, it is normal to want to put your child in preschool, music classes, art and dance, karate, gymnastics, etc, all before the age of 5! Not to mention, perhaps private school for the first 5 years. All of this requires money.

One last participant said that her mother probably called herself, 'bored'. Staying home was a sacrifice and this young mother wasn't sure it was something she could ever do. She thinks that she will continue to work part time after her first baby is born. As we speak, she is home with her first baby, still not at the six- week mark. Her story is yet to be told.

One Stay-at-Home Dad married late in life (42 years old) and was actually in a position to not have to work the rest of his life. That is to say that he had enough for his retirement as a single person, but not enough for a family to retire on. When his wife, who was highly successful and on an upward mobility career ladder became pregnant, they mutually agreed that he would be the Stay-at- Home Dad. It worked for the first year, barely. Then depression set in. He was in therapy and on medication. When the second child came along, they hired a full-time nanny and he simply picked and chose what he was willing to do and what he was not. This man is a great role model for mothers. He is able to say no, no and no. He never even thinks that he should be able to do all that is required of him. He became depressed and sought professional help. A nanny was instantly installed. Days off created, and weekends to himself. Amazing.

Isn't it interesting that both women and men agree that parenting is the most significant and difficult job on the planet? How many of you have husbands that actually want you stay home, particularly if they are able to single-handedly command a decent and sufficient paycheck and career? What is this all about? Is it true that men want their wives to stay home and raise the children? The number of men who prefer moms to be at home is probably staggering. And if this is true, is it also not true that men have a role in not only requesting and preferring this arrangement, but more or equally as important a role in giving this decision the merit, respect, and daily appreciation that it deserves? How many men could stay home? How many Stay-at-Home Dads are there anyway? Do they not suffer depression? You can guess that the answer is yes.

Our society's perception is that by nature and socialization women are set up for second-class citizenship and backseat importance. Granted we have organizations such as La Leche League and the well-known Lamaze classes to help prepare and support women as they venture into motherhood. However as far as maternal support, this is only the tip of the iceberg. Much, much more is needed to provide adequate armor for the great leap from career into the abyss of motherhood.

It is up to your generation to create the image and the roles that either Stay-at-Home Mom or part time Mom demands. Proud moments like watching your toddler advance to the next class in gymnastics, being the bravest, the most timid, the most verbal, the cutest, the biggest eyes, the best smile, saying the most adoring things possible are not hard to come by. Children easily melt your heart away day after day, night after night. And while these are the moments that are shared by your husbands, close friends, there is no current reality show, no media rap focusing on the positive aspects of motherhood. It leaves the role model up to you. Give us one. Give us a *Million Dollar Mommy*. Maybe a new reality show is in the making!

# ~ 4 ~

## Climbing the Ladder or Rocking the Cradle
### The Struggle to Juggle

Climbing the corporate ladder or rocking the cradle describes one of the many challenges for the new millennium Mom. According to a Newsweek article written by Judith Warner, the craziness associated with motherhood for our generation is 'nothing less than a nationwide epidemic'. Perhaps you have been thinking that you were the only one, well, one of the only mothers out there who felt stressed, tired, depressed, disappointed and confused most of the time. It appears that many mothers today are not prepared to be taken away by motherhood, in fact, most are probably very ill prepared for it.

According to the survey results, most of the mothers reported that they thought that they would work either part- or full-time after their children were born. Many of the women who thought that they would work full time actually work part-time or have quit their outside work entirely. A few entrepreneurial women have either purchased businesses so that they could work their children into their schedule, or have begun home-based businesses. Aside from a change in the work place, our survey participant Moms reported what they thought that their lives would look like after children, and what their lives actually do look like now that they have children. One hundred percent (100%) of the Moms surveyed indicated that they had no idea that their lives would change as dramatically as they did. Some of the Moms knew they were in for a life change, but none of them reported that their lives post-children looked anything close to what they thought it would. WOW!

Women and mothers of the current generation have spent a great deal of time and energy developing identities through their careers. And when those identities via the workplace are taken away and/ or significantly changed, a state of panic and immense inner struggle can set in.

*Nobody told me that I wouldn't be myself anymore, or that it would feel like I didn't have a life anymore. And even if someone had, I'm not sure in my career-oriented mind that I would have accepted or even listened to such information. I had no idea how to create a new me, but that is exactly what I had to do in order to find peace with my new role.*

A planner by nature this woman doesn't like surprises or having loose ends. Certainly she didn't realize that she would have to create a new self, or the importance of doing so. More specifically, she probably didn't have the tools at her disposal to do it. Is it any wonder that her world was turned upside down? Mothering is all about the unexpected, surprises and loose ends ad nauseam. Being a Mom is hard. Losing her hard-fought career identity because she became a Mom was maddening. To this woman, a professional identity was of the utmost importance. She was not raised to be satisfied with the role of 'just a Mom'. Listen to the web she wove.

*Many of my personal and professional expectations from life were formed early on. I thought that I could make a career for myself as a writer in the third grade, and even wrote a horror story to tell my class. When I presented this idea to my Mom, she laughed and said that it was nearly impossible to make a living as a writer. From that day on, I decided that I would do something practical with my life and would become a doctor. I was very good at school and was determined to make a go of it. However, when I was in college, I told my Dad that I wanted to be a doctor like him* and he told me that I'd never make it through medical school. Deflated and discouraged I finished college with a degree in English, after two full years of pre-medical studies. Although my parents didn't intentionally shape my thoughts about what I could do or not do, they obviously had a far greater impact than they realized.

Red flag! Hopefully the Generation X of mothers (and fathers) knows that it is their job to believe in their child's dreams and ambitions. A young child is continuously looking to the parents to find out if they are okay. Are their ideas okay? Are they good enough? Smart enough? Strong enough? And in the above scenario not only did the mother laugh at her daughter's grand idea, but it is also probable that the mother never told her that it was okay be a Mom and just a Mom. Her mother is not a bad parent, just an uninformed parent.

*After graduating from college, and deflecting the ever-present assumption that you could only be a teacher with an English degree, I set out to create a professional life for myself. I worked at a financial institution for a year. I then moved to another state. I didn't have a job at the time, but knew that I could find one. The job that I landed would shape my professional life in a way that I could never have dreamed.*

*Just before I started my family, I branched out with a few of my colleagues and began our own small consulting business. I told my partners at the onset that I was only in it for about two years, and then I would be done because I wanted to do something else with my life.*

*Although it was hard to part with the golden handcuffs i.e., a healthy annual salary, that my consulting career had equipped me with, after four years of being a partner in a small firm, and two children, it was really time to let go. It was going fine, but I didn't want "fine", I wanted something more. It never occurred to me that raising my children would be enough.*

*Not having a paycheck was a real blow to my self-esteem in ways that I never imagined. I had saved up some money to get me through this very event, but all of the sudden it seemed so insufficient. I felt guilty not working for a paycheck, although I was doing the bulk of the child-care and the domestic duties. It was very foreign to me to be out of the workforce, and felt a panic to hurry up and find something else to do. My husband assured me that I could (and should) take some time and figure out what it was that I really wanted to do.*

Note this lady's language. She was panicking to find something to do. Caring for her baby and maintaining the home while all consuming still left her thinking that she had to DO something MORE, ELSE, and that *something* was defined by a paycheck. Of equal concern and importance is the fact that this woman, 'saved up some money' to get her through raising her baby. Her husband tries to comfort her by telling her to take some time to figure out what she really wanted to do. Did she really want to have a baby, and then have another one, or not? Yes. Of Course. But does she want to do something else too? Isn't it odd that even though she had and was caring for those babies, she still did not feel like what she was doing was legitimate? Does any one get told that when you have a baby you have already made lots of decisions? When you have a baby more happens than your body changing. More happens than just another being in the house. Having a baby makes more life decisions for you than probably any other act does.

*I needed to make some serious changes. I wasn't happy, I was drained of all energy, my husband had become the enemy, and I deduced that I needed to change my career goals. I thought that if I got my career in order, everything else would fall into place. It didn't dawn on me that there were larger issues at play. It wasn't my job, or lack of job that was the problem. It was a much deeper issue. I had lost myself in the process of becoming a mother. All things that I used to identify myself to the outside world were now gone. Everything I'd worked for, hoped for, planned for, was stripped from me as I entered the realm of motherhood. The flip side was that I did not regret having my children. I certainly did not want anyone else to be the primary caregiver; but there I was a floundering, hopeless shell of a being, kicking and screaming about the injustices of the universe and feeling like I was walking around with a scarlet L (loser) on my forehead.*

She feels like she has lost her self. Isn't that odd? And isn't it a common feeling for new mothers? What is wrong with this picture? Why don't you feel like you have gained another incredible identity, an identity that far outweighs and surpasses the identity of Account Executive or Vice President of Marketing or Creative Director? Because we have become such a money conscious and financially responsible society (and we mean our target group of women), without a paycheck, we think and feel that we are really less than we are.

According to *The First Sex*, "...there is a great deal of evidence that women are more inclined to try to balance work with family than men are...more working women than men thought their career was too big a sacrifice; it wasn't worth it...every time you would miss a child's birthday, a school concert or a parent teacher discussion, you'd feel the tug. As a rule, women are not as willing as men to stay late in the office, travel constantly, skip school events, entertain clients in the evening or relocate, sacrificing their family lives and their personal interests for their careers. Many more women drop out of high salaried jobs if they feel their work jeopardized their ability to rear their children."

"From the strictly evolutionary perspective this feminine proclivity to balance work and family makes sense; nothing is more important to a woman's future than the survival of her children. Men have opportunities to breed throughout their lives. But women can bear only a few babies. They are obliged to rear these precious creatures if they are to spread their DNA into perpetuity. This is nature's law."

*I don't really want to engage in a huge career outside the home because I really value the time I do get to spend with my children, and it's important to both me and my husband that one of us is around most of the time. So, at least for the moment, I have to do something that I can accomplish in a few hours during the day, that I can put off if I need to because a child is sick, and something that I can do primarily from home. Not totally unrealistic, but it really is something that I have to create for myself. Of course there are days when I really wish that I could escape to the office, but I find that I miss my kids when they aren't around. Crazy huh?*

> "When I am at work, I want to be home with my kids.
> When I am home, I want to be at work."

This woman finds no peace in either domain. It is extremely frustrating to never be at peace with where you are. It is crazy making to want to cut yourself in half. It is also exhausting. Make a sound decision about career and home, take responsibility for it, and embrace the experience. Be present where you are. Find ways to make your choice as good as possible. As older mothers have said in their infinite wisdom, "you never get these years back. They are only little once." At the time when children are little experiencing that children are 'little only once', is hard to keep remembering. However, experience teaches you at a core and gut level. Being a parent in your early twenties does not give you the emotional maturity that mothers having their babies in their thirties have. In your early twenties you haven't lived long enough to realize that life really does have stages. The curious paradox here is that mothers in their thirties have had lots of experiences such as: college degrees, careers, multiple relationships, even for some a previous marriage. So wouldn't it appear that they would be primed and ready to stay home and do the home thing???? Yes, possibly, if in fact staying home was a positive experience! And, maybe more so if major financial and self-esteem issues weren't compromised.

One male client shared that his girlfriend who wanted to get married and have a family actually believed that she could have a child and then every other day he would be in charge and then she would be in charge...or maybe it was every other week. As if a switch could be turned off and on. Okay pass the football, now it is your turn and I am going to go check out. What this naïve young woman did not understand is that the mother's clock, mother's hearing, mother's instincts never get turned off. Even if it isn't your night to get up with the baby, you still are the one that hears the baby, nudges the Dad and then lies there wondering if he can really change, feed, soothe and get the baby back to sleep. If you know how to do this, to emotionally check out, then perhaps you too should write a book! Is it any wonder that the women in our survey refer to being a Mom as a 24/7 assignment?

Your own mother's experience is powerful in your decision to stay at home or to keep working full time. One participant told the following story. She recalled from her childhood hearing her mother often discuss how hard it was when she was a single working mom raising a child by herself. When her mom remarried, she was able to stay home and did so! Interestingly, when this participant decided to walk away from her upwardly mobile career, she found herself conflicted. She had heard it was a luxury to stay home -- yet she loved her career and really had intended to do both. She shared that it was hard and mostly for the first six months of adjustment. They, she and her husband, agreed that she really did want to stay home and raise the babies. She really began to see this role as the most important role she could be choosing.

Both she and her husband had positive mother role models, and knew that it was worth it. In other words, she had permission to stay home. Her executive and organizational skills have not gone to waste. This participant runs her house just like she ran her department when she was in the work force. She is definitely the CEO and the COO and the CIO of the home front. She brings dignity and respect to her role as a Stay-at-Home Mom.

There are some necessary ingredients to adjusting to your Mom role with pride. First and foremost, guard your path. You are the only one walking in your shoes. Come to grips with your role as a mother because once you become one, you are a Mom forever. Then, and only then, can you make intelligent decisions about your career. Spend the time it takes to honestly answer these questions:

What is your job as mother?
What is your role?
What is expected of you?
Who do you turn to for advice in being a Mom?
Who is your role model? Why?
What is your image of a Mother?
Does the image fit what you admire?
What do you want to 'look like' as a Mom?
How do you want to dress?
Do you want to play up or play down the role?
What privileges come with being a Mom?
Are you willing to create some privileges other than Mother's Day?
What is the cost of being a Mom?
How are you going to be compensated?
How can you make your image as a Mother a powerful positive person?

Answers to the above questions can really only be accurate when you actually become a mother. It will continue to evolve the first few years. Something happens to you, something that no one can really describe. In fact, no one can know what will happen for certain due to the fact that life changes forever. You change forever. Emotional parts of you that you didn't know existed come to life. Suddenly buttons get pushed that you didn't know you had. For example, did you know that your self-esteem would get challenged? Did you know that your self worth would be in question? Did you know that feelings of self-pity, and tremendous responsibility would lie on your shoulders at times like bricks and mortar? Did you know that when you would watch a movie and a child were injured that you would identify with that mother's pain? The questions and surprises go on and on. The point is that as these brand new phenomena, feelings, experiences pour down on you, it is normal.

Stand tall! Self- esteem need not and must not take a slap in the face. Claim loudly and proudly that you are a MOM. Feel good about it. Own the title. If you are proud of your position as a mother, then it will make it easier to get the support of your husband. If you are ashamed or feel less than a complete person, you open up the door to be treated as such.

*As far as self-respect is concerned, I have to say that being a mother is an awesome responsibility, and I drew on strengths that I didn't even know I had. I think that in a lot of ways, becoming a mother has forced me to focus on my own personal priorities and values in a way that I was taking for granted before. I think about things that I would like to teach my children as well as the things that I don't want to teach my children. I talk to my husband about what our joint values are. I respect myself more for a variety of reasons, one of which is not engaging in self-destructive behavior. I want to be a good parent and spouse and think that by doing a lot of introspection that I am accomplishing these goals.*

*As far as my husband is concerned, I think that he probably respects me more now that I am the mother of his children. I don't think that I've ever really asked him the question, and maybe I will, but I think that's where he stands.*

One concept that will help you feel good about your role as a mother is to take the role seriously. The happiest Moms are those who see themselves as the CEO of the home. They take charge and run their homes like a great ocean liner. They are highly organized, efficient and know how and when to delegate. These empowered Moms know that is okay to use their support system to help them care for their children.

One thing is certain. You never ever get the early child-rearing years back. Never. With each child you only go through the first few years once. This is not rocket science but women forget. Women, being so overwhelmed, forget that there is time. Time to have another professional life in their forties or fifties or even sixties. If you are going through the early child rearing years in your thirties, consider pausing your career and taking it up again when they are in school. The Stay-at-Home Moms that finally get all the children in school, laugh at the time that they have on their hands...remember when your first one went to preschool two mornings a week...and you had 2-3 full hours to your self? Wow! There is time. There is time to do many lives and make many choices.

# ~ 5 ~

# Self-esteem

The transition from a career, title and paycheck to being a mother, part time or full time is one of those rites of passage not without extreme challenge to the psyche. Women describe with sorrow the transition from being a 'breadwinner to bread-maker'; from a focus on a portfolio to a focus on pampers; feelings of the status change from CEO to Cinderella. All the aforementioned imply a step down, a less attractive description and often a feeling of damaged self-esteem. Low self-esteem can easily turn into depression.

Depression goes along with new motherhood. It even has a name, postpartum depression. And it can be very unnerving to have feelings of depression, i.e., helplessness and hopelessness after being a successful career person out in the world. Furthermore, you may not have realized how much of yourself would be lost taking care of a newborn baby. Your once busy, important, deadline-oriented schedule becomes a blur of feedings, diaper changes, and sleep interruption.

*You suddenly feel like you don't have anything tangible to show for your efforts during the course of 24 hours, and just being able to take a shower feels like a major accomplishment. After the first few days, you can really begin to have some serious doubts about who you are and what you have done with your life.*

Many of the author's books cited in the bibliography have addressed the issue of self-esteem and the loss thereof. More than just losing your self-esteem, though, you can actually lose your self in child-caring tasks. One of our participants puts it best in suggesting that the title of our book should be called, I HAVEN'T SHOWERED SINCE TUESDAY! In Andrea J. Buchanan's Book, "Mother Shock" there is an entire chapter called The Invisible Woman. Once you become a mother, you understand exactly what that means. You're treated differently by the outside world, your own thoughts and actions are forced into the realm of your newborn baby, and you may feel like you don't really exist except to change diapers, feed your baby and change clothing (both the baby's and yours). This alternate existence is nothing short of alienating and many new mothers wonder *what happened to me?*

*Me, where do I go?*
*Me, myself, and I*
*I wonder why?*

*Mommy gimme a drink,*
*Mommy tie my shoes,*
*Mommy, can Timmy come over?*

*At night time I sit and I stare*
*Alone, wondering*
*Where did I go? Where am I?*

The above poem expresses the loneliness and lost feelings of self, experienced as a young mother 30 years ago. It's from a Mom whose only aspiration in life was to be a Mom. 30 years later, these moments of loss and loneliness are still being expressed and experienced by new mothers.

*Self-esteem has not ever been my strong suit. Although I realized early on that I was intelligent, perhaps more so than some, I never felt like that mattered nearly as much as being pencil thin, having a fabulous up-to-date wardrobe, and being drop-dead gorgeous, all items that I didn't possess. I can say that I've never, ever felt so unattractive and weight-conscious as I did during each of my two pregnancies and immediately thereafter. I can remember sobbing while looking down at my flabby abdomen after giving birth to my son, wondering how in the world I would ever get it back into pre-pregnancy shape…and even in that shape, I didn't like the way it looked. I can't tell you what a toll the whole morphing body experience took on my self-esteem. I felt positively enormous.*

Some of you may love being pregnant. Pregnancy can make you feel beautiful. It can make you feel like a woman for the first time in your life. You may feel full of sexuality and femininity. You can feel proud and fortunate to have very little morning sickness or lethargy. For the first time your breasts fill a bra. You might like that. It may sound silly, but for a teenage girl who waits and waits for her breasts to grow so that she can be like everyone else, having full breasts can be fun, fulfilling and a beautiful thing. You many even love the breast-feeding experience.

Or you may hate it. You may hate the weight and hate being pregnant. You may not like anything about it and dread getting pregnant again. You may feel sluggish, always tired, and unattractive. Your back hurts, your ankles are swollen and all in all, pregnancy can be a miserable thing.

It is uncertain what makes one pregnancy an easier physiological experience than another, but it goes without saying that if you have a bad physical experience, emotionally it is going to be really rough. If you have questionable self-esteem issues prior to pregnancy, it can go either way. Loving being pregnant and having a great experience can boost you self-esteem. A lousy experience can take away and damage the good self-esteem experienced prior to pregnancy.

Self-esteem is a huge issue. According to Webster's dictionary, the definition of self-esteem is… 'a confidence and satisfaction of 'oneself'. With the keyword "oneself", which self do we mean? The career self? The wife self? The lover self? The child self, daughter, sister, friend? Most of our survey participants responded that their self-esteem had improved as a result of being a Mom, but there was a consistent underlying tone that the career self, the woman self, and the independent being self took a beating. One of the biggest adjustments to your self-esteem and motherhood is taking on an unglamorous, unsophisticated role.

*"I had a very important career and a lot of responsibility...it was particularly hard for me (to choose to stay at home full time) because I did define myself by my career and in part by the money I brought to the table. As far as career downsizing is concerned, I didn't feel like I had an equal voice because I wasn't contributing financially to the family picture, whereas I was in a large way pre-kids. Even when I was working part-time and doing almost all of the childcare, I didn't feel like it was adequate. For one thing, I have been told, and frequently, not to let a man provide for you financially because then he owns you. Terrifying. Also, I am the product of a very hard-working single Mom, and it just doesn't feel right not to work in some sort of significant occupation.*

Not really too surprising is the fact that many women who have titles and command big salaries at first glance are locked into the concept that their net worth equals their self worth. After all, that is what we as a capitalistic nation teach. Money defines who we are. Climbing the corporate ladder is what we do. We want to get ahead and we want to make more money doing so...vertical not horizontal moves. Is it any wonder that someone in this setting would not really be able to get a grip on having a baby as a vertical move, let alone a horizontal one? In the corporate world it could be viewed as a death sentence to your career. Even though it is against the law to fire someone because they are pregnant, my guess is that being pregnant does create some very gray lines for upper management.

*"In theory, I would like to accept that title (of Stay at-Home-Mom) but I feel it is underrated in our society, but by not working outside of the home, I tend to feel like I am selling myself short and letting down women who have fought so hard for us to have more choices outside of the home"?*

This woman is clearly conflicted, tugged in two opposing directions.

Do you have more or less respect for yourself now that you are a Mom? One woman responded that she was certainly proud of being a good Mom and trying to put some good people out in the world. However, she was feeling insecure about approaching 40 and being out of the workforce for so many years. She confessed that she sometimes feels like she is taking the easy way out by not working at least part time and this makes her feel bad about herself. Now the interesting observation about this comment is that she also rates the job of being a Mom at a difficulty of 10 (on a scale from 1 to 10). She goes on to say that life is more stressful (ranked a 10 on a scale of 1-10) and she has experienced symptoms of depression since staying at home. She does not pamper herself. She does not have regular date nights with her husband and calls herself overweight. She says that she should have more respect for herself being a Stay-at-Home Mom but the fact remains that she does not.

Self-respect and self-esteem go hand in hand. If you were able to get both respect and self-esteem at work, then that is great. Did you take it away with you if you decided to be a stay-at-home Mom? Did your esteem and respect lose any ground in the transition?

Several points can boost and be factors in women feeling good about themselves and having good self-esteem. Spouses can really play a dramatic part in validating the honor of being a Mom. Verbalizing, talking about how great Mom is can be powerful in teaching and modeling respect for the role. Many women commented that their spouses admitted that, "Oh, yeah, I could never do what she does" and "Oh yeah, I definitely prefer that she is at home." When asked how often they verbalize this, actually speak the words, what they do and what their wives hear doesn't match up. In other words, Dad was quick to admit the difficulty of staying at home, in some cases the impossibility to do so himself. He assumed that she knew that. The women that had the easiest transition were the ones that made the necessary adjustments but also unequivocally felt more respected and honored by their husbands for doing the job that was most taxing and with the most powerful consequences. These men and fathers were not stingy in their gratitude and attentiveness that they lavished on their wives. Maybe our favorite Grandpa John was right with his advice to his grandsons when they got married...he told them, 'Happy Wives, Happy Lives'. He learned early on that if his wife was happy with her home, her house, her role as mother and housewife, then life was good. He truly believed that she ran the house. It was her domain and whatever she wanted and needed; he would do his best to provide. And he told her so and told his children as well. Wow! Imagine that!

Self-esteem as we discuss it in this book, is about focusing on your self-esteem as a mother. Good self-esteem would imply having confidence, satisfaction, feeling proud of your role as a mother and wearing the label with dignity. Self-esteem can come from your own perceptions and thoughts that you are telling yourself. For example, if you tell yourself, 'I feel like a chauffeur, at everyone's beck and call,' you will fill used. Or if you tell yourself, 'I am so fortunate that I don't have to work 9-5 and can be around to pick him up and be on the inside of what is going on with his little friend, teacher or coach,' you will feel valued. If instead of making another meal, you find a way to make 3 meals at once, you will feel clever and ahead of the game. Negotiating with your spouse cooking and clean up duties, and doing whatever it takes to not feel like the martyr, the victim, the slave will ease the bumps in the road of motherhood.

One mother with older children shared in hindsight the following:

*"Even though I knew that I had been emotionally and physically worn out and emotionally hijacked during my kids younger years, I had no idea the toll everything had taken on me personally until I finally had the opportunity to really get away for several days. I had taken on the new role as Mom, juggling part time work, taking on a new business, resenting the relatively small role my husband seemed to be taking, and the role of 24-hour caretaker (even when working part time, their care was on my mind and my responsibility 24/7). Oh, and in the process, I also moved to a developing country! I actually thought I was doing ok balancing all of this until this trip made me realize that I had lost myself in the process.*

*When my kids were about 6 and 3, I took a 5-day trip far away with some close girlfriends. During that trip my close friends made comments like "You're so funny", "You're always so active and into exercise", and*

*"You inspire me". And when some harmless flirting made me realize that I could, once again, feel attractive, I finally put it all together. I was re-discovering ME. My friends made those kinds of comments because they hadn't seen that in me since pre-kids. And, I certainly hadn't felt attractive since before pregnancy. I rediscovered ME, and most of all I realized that I liked ME and did not want to lose ME. Sure it's one thing to be Mom, part-time-work juggler, business owner, wife, and 24-hour caregiver - but if I lose ME in the process, then a huge piece is missing, and I'm not nearly as good in any of those roles. The best part is that when I came back from that trip, I was a lot more fun, I was a lot better to/for my husband and kids, and I had the goal of keeping ME to hold on to. It was a wonderful discovery, and I believe I wouldn't have lost so much of ME if I had taken more time to myself, delegated the Mom responsibilities better, and had demanded more time for my husband and I to spend alone, not talking about the kids or the business, but just laughing and even flirting like we did before kids. I've since made it a priority to get away by myself on a trip with friends at least once a year. It has made a huge difference.*

Your self-esteem will definitely be in the toilet if you do not take time for yourself first. It is assumed that you are supposed to and assumed that you don't because time is the one thing that you are short on. This is the same argument that people make when financial planners tell people; you have to pay yourself first...not last. Because if you pay yourself last, there is never any left over to pay yourself with. But if you pay yourself first, somehow, some magical way, everything else gets paid. So too it is with taking time for you first, not last. If you are last on the list, surely you will never, absolutely never find the time. That is a promise. But if you make time for yourself first, miraculously all else will fall into place.

Women by nature and nurture are geared to give to others, put others needs first, wait their turn, and not be selfish. There is a certain amount of token praise that women receive for these traits. Having them won't necessarily create a healthy motherhood experience. What if you could hang on to your sanity, your self worth, your dignity, your sexuality, your power, and your pride? Would you not be a more peaceful mother? What if you put your self-care at the top of the list?

Pour your cup full first. Keep your own cup full, so that you can keep giving. Too many mothers are running around with too many empty cups for too long. Too many mothers that do not have good self-esteem, particularly in the role of mothering, have only copied and mastered martyrs before them. Martyrs do not make for happy, healthy, positive, energizing people. Perhaps in the biblical sense martyrs are a good thing, but in the mothering sense in the new millennium, martyrs spell disaster, depression and total depletion.

When you feel used, not valued and sleep deprived, and if you find yourself keeping score, resentment will build and your husband becomes the enemy. Resentment is a setup for destruction. You self-destruct by depriving yourself of passion and romance. You spend time determining and documenting the many ways that you are being wronged. You self-destruct by picking fights. You may even find yourself putting energy into being right, not happy, and trying to win a game that you have decided to play unbeknownst to your spouse or perhaps yourself. Oftentimes, husband bashing becomes a comforting past time with your girlfriends, or anyone who will listen, your hairdresser, grocer, etc.

One such mother left her newborn baby and the toddler for three days with her husband to prove a point. Good idea or not? Her motive was revenge and vindictiveness. It can be argued that he did get to have one-on-one time with his children. Maybe it made him more sensitive, then again maybe the baby cried all night, and maybe the mother's point wasn't made at all.

Another woman kept the exact hours of the time that she spent with the children. If the children's father did something that was not directly work-related, the woman made sure that she spent the exact amount of time doing something without the kids. The point was not to improve her self-esteem, but to teach him a lesson. This creates competition not cooperation and is a very adversarial position to take. So if you are keeping score, there is something else going on i.e., not feeling validated, feeling overwhelmed or maybe just bone tired. Some Moms are still resentful years later if they didn't resolve their issues. Do what you can to make certain that you do not become a bitter, resentful, depressed, or (dare say) desperate housewife.

# ~ 6 ~

## Captain the Mother Ship

Remember how stimulating it was to be moved from the center cubicle to a space with a window? Remember how more efficient you were when you had all the right tools at your disposal? The laptop, the palm pilot, the blackberry. Remember how proud you were and how awesome it was to decorate and buff out your workspace, just for you, personally, individually? Well, so too, your home. Even more so if you choose to stay home full time. Sorry Dads, you may really hate this but what Mom needs to run the house, Mom should have at the first opportunity possible.

Take turns with your husband of being in charge of any project or decision. The rule is if you are in charge, then he supports you and agrees to your decisions, thus consequences. Vice versa, if he is in charge of the shopping for food for example, then you are grateful, appreciative and learn to cook with what he brings home!

Take charge. Whoever is the stay at home parent, be in charge. Bear in mind that even if both parents are working outside the home, the Mom will typically be more than 99% in charge of the home. We are not talking about becoming bossy or dictatorial, simply be assertive. Command the ship. Be the leader. Sometimes we cannot afford the big house on the hill. However, wherever your home is, honor your space. Be able to be proud of where you live. Do the best you can with what you've got. Make it your castle. That means clean out the clutter; throw out the trash; fix what's broken; donate what you don't use. Organize. Organize. Organize. Make the beds each day. Hang up the clothes. Create the schedules. Have a system. And if organizing is not your forte, hire a professional organizer. It will be worth every penny spent.

# ~ 7 ~

## Create Your Own Personal Perks

The survey participants were asked if they had established 'sick days' for themselves as Stay-at-Home Moms. Most all laughed and said things like, "Yeah, sure! Real funny! Is that really an option?"

The reason for this question is yet another question. Why don't you establish sick days, vacation days and personal leave? You can you know. It is true that no one is going to give it to you. But that doesn't mean that you cannot create it. In fact, do this! Step up to the plate and determine what you need in order for you to not feel used and abused and undervalued. When you feel like life is unfair, it is easy to keep score. Mothers almost always feel under appreciated and undervalued. Part of this lies in your hands. Start appreciating your self, your role, your importance and others will follow. All that society has done for Moms is give them a one-day holiday of recognition. It is called Mother's Day. Is that all you get? One day a year? How absurd is that?

## Time Off

- One hour a day; one evening a week; one whole Saturday 8-5

Any entrepreneur or person that works from home, and lives to tell about it, learns the hard way that days off have to be scheduled. Office hours must be set. Otherwise you are fair play, always working, always available, because no one else is punching the time clock for you. Is it any different for Mom? Don't you work from home? Don't you work the back of the clock? Don't you always have the graveyard shift, just in case? Who is looking out for you? You, and you alone. It is okay. It is your responsibility to take care of yourself, so that you can take care of everyone else. Days off do just that.

## Date Nights and Rendezvous

- Minimum 2 per month; could also be a breakfast date; a lunch date.

Date Night. Think about it. Remember when? Remember when you were footloose and fancy-free? Remember, looking forward to the end of the 'workweek'. Letting your hair down, going out, chilling out and appreciating good music, fine art, and adult conversation?

Go somewhere with your husband for twenty-four hours…. even Friday at 5pm (yes, miss supper, baths, bedtime and breakfast) until Saturday at 11am. What this really means is skip responsibilities. Skip the part where you have to have three bites, just three bites of the newly introduced broccoli trees. Skip the part where rubber ducky is going to go for a swim and get his feathers shampoo-ed. Skip the part of one more story, one more song, prayers and brushing your teeth.

*My husband and I are now committed to having a date night whenever we can. This helps keep me centered as more than a Mom and gives me some of the "me" and "us" time that my relationship needs to survive and grow. This in turn, has created a renewed interest in the romantic side of our relationship.*

Create, insist and request 'date nights' on a regular basis, minimum every other week. Set boundaries around the date night or date lunch, such as not talking about the children. Agree not to call each other

Mom and Dad but remembering and using your own loving pet names (sweetheart and lover) for one another.

Have some adult awake time with your spouse...sans children. In general, create a bedtime schedule and routine whereby all children, especially under the age of 4 are in bed at a consistent time that gives you and your spouse at least 1-2 hrs of adult time before you go to bed (unless of course you are nursing, and that is different). In addition to creating adult time with your spouse, you'll be doing right by your children. There are many articles and books written about the need for young children to sleep, and many are reportedly sleep-deprived. Do yourself and everyone else a favor and make it a non-negotiable part of the nighttime routine.

Moms and Dads must continue to work on their relationship when the kids are young. Too often Moms ignore this advice and become 100% focused on the children, and may even become nervous or agitated at the thought of spending one-on-one time with their husbands. Do try to stay connected with your husband, your children will be gone sooner than you realize. Won't it be great to look forward to hanging out and growing old with your spouse instead of wondering what to do with him when the children are gone?

Personal perks such as the two mentioned above are a good thing. Add your own. Ask other Moms what they do for personal perks. It's okay, promise.

# ~ 8 ~

## *Know Your Issues, Do Your Homework*

In addition to the historical and cultural view of motherhood causing confusion, a woman's own childhood issues may cloud her logic. These types of issues are often associated with how a person was parented. It is fascinating to observe how your own unresolved childhood issues will surface as soon as you become a parent.

You may not know how to take care of yourself. You may only know how to do what you learned as a little girl. Don't bug Daddy. He's tired. Make sure you don't upset him. No arguing, make home a peaceful place so that he wants to come home. Do it all and be grateful.

Many of our survey respondents indicated that they knew that their mothers felt that staying at home with their children was a sacrifice. Some of our respondents indicated that their own mothers had given up lucrative or interesting careers to stay at home with their children, and not always by choice.

*Prior to my parents' divorce, my Mom was a Stay-at-Home Mom.*
*I don't remember much of the time that my dad was part of the family*

*when we were an intact family because he was a physician. I don't really remember him being around much at all. His role in my life was very intermittent, and mostly full of broken promises.*

*After my parents divorced, and we became a broken family, my Mom returned to work full time. Although I don't recall doing without the basic necessities, I do know that it was a struggle for my Mom to make financial ends meet. I hear her tell stories of how much she enjoyed being around her little kids, how we made her laugh, and how much she loved us. From what I have heard her say, her sacrifice was twofold, she sacrificed herself to stay in a crummy marriage so that she could stay at home with us when we were very young; and after her divorce, she sacrificed time with us to provide for us.*

*I can remember doing a project in my third grade class where we were supposed to do a collage of what we wanted to be when we grew up. I chose to be a hang-glider. I'm not sure why I considered that a profession, or why it appealed to me at the time. I was really surprised to find out that most of the girls in my class had 'housewife' collages. I guess with my Mom working all of the time, I didn't think that girls grew up to stay at home with the kids.*

*What I learned from my mother as far as parenting was concerned was that it wasn't easy, you could not rely on men to help you out, and you had to work your butt off in order to provide the basic necessities. The useful skills that I learned growing up in my broken family were a fierce sense of independence, how to save money, and the innate knowledge that I would survive and could always find a way to pay the bills.*

*My mother also modeled to me that after all the children had gone and left the nest, then it was okay to put herself first and to do the things that she loved to do. She began running, started riding bicycles for exercise, and she loved to travel and did so to exotic places.*

Would it stand to reason that this woman would not know how to incorporate a Dad into the parenting picture and that she would expect that she had to do everything herself?

It is easy to see that the childhood experience truly shaped this person's role of motherhood. It appears from our surveys that the women that had positive happy Stay-at-Home Moms have an easier transition into choosing that path. If you're one of those mothers who had a mother who wanted to stay at home, but couldn't, you could carry resentment and disappointment into your parenting. It can also be noted that the women who have role models that resented being a housewife and Stay-at-Home Mom have some unspoken promise to not make that mistake. Ironically, most of the participants did not come from professional mothers with careers. Perhaps this is a result of the times, the limited participant list, or some other explanation. It seems that there is a proverbial struggle and unspoken dialogue about how to truly do what you want, i.e., stay at home full time, keep the career going, or juggle part time work. Looking at your childhood can help uncover some of the possible reasons why you choose what you choose.

A client, years ago vowed that she would be available to her child, if she ever had one, because her own mother was never around. And of course what happened was an extreme overreaction of this mother's part. The following story occurred in a residential adolescent hospital and involved both mother and daughter. The daughter was a 16 year-old, a straight-A student, all of her school years until the prior year to her in-house treatment. She had begun to get D's and F's; act out with drugs, sex, and rock and roll and in general became a most unpleasant young lady. When an initial intake was done, she confessed that she was sick and tired of her mother. She hated her mother. In fact, what she really hated was her mother's bumper sticker boasting that 'My Daughter is a Straight A Student'. The girl claimed that the grades didn't even belong to her anymore. Her mother stole them by bragging to everyone, being obnoxious at the parent teacher conferences, high school plays, events and anything social. The girl had wanted to get back and have something to call her own. So she turned in good grades for tattoos, a foul mouth, ragged clothing and poor grades. Her mother was shocked, overwhelmed and at a total loss as to what had gone wrong when she knew in fact that she had given her daughter everything and anything that she wanted.

When interviewed, the mother was in total disbelief about what had gone wrong. Why had her daughter gotten herself into such a downward spiral? When asked about her own childhood growing up, she confessed that she was raised by a single Mom, an only child and basically raised herself. Her mother was never there for her, resented being a Mom, having a child and she never missed a day alluding to the fact. This mother in treatment vowed that if she ever found herself pregnant, she would worship her child, love her intensely and always, always be there for her. And while this mother's intentions were sincere, she ended up suffocating her own child and literally smothering her with love that was too much. She did not honor the child's need for autonomy and independence. She had horrible boundaries. She gave her the love that she needed but also the love that she needed her own mother to have given her. It was simply a case of too much of the wrong kind of love. Double timing is what she was doing. Doing time for her child and doing time trying to heal her own childhood need to be mothered.

The biggest single hint that there is more than just the child's needs' going on is when you find yourself (or others point out) that your reaction, your behavior is too much. When the intensity level does not match the intensity of the situation, it usually means that a button has been pushed. That button could indicate unresolved childhood issues.

Everyone has issues. Truly they do. And your children will have issues as well. Some people call these 'quirks' 'idiosyncrasies'. For example, being a control freak can damage your child's emotional health. Being afraid of your own shadow can thwart your child's freedom to explore, take risks, and find adventure. Don't shove your own restrictions and hang ups onto your children. The more you know about yourself and where you are emotionally healthy and where you might need some work, the better environment you will be able to give your children. Remember, they are always watching you. Your children see and absorb much more that you realize.

Parental teamwork can flourish and benefit the children if you and your husband 'back off' if a button for one of you is getting pushed and allow the other parent to step in. Psychotherapy can be extremely helpful to adults and allow them to parent much more effectively. If you have damage from your own childhood, and many people do, do your homework; get into therapy, preferably before you start your family. The healthier you are emotionally, the easier and more effective you will be parenting your children.

# ~ 9 ~

## The Elephants in the Room
### Money Matters (because it really does)

The financial worth of motherhood is a force to be reckoned with. Back in the early 70's a book that never made it into print about being a mother was entitled the "Housewife: The Invisible Occupation". Today relatively few women choose the title of housewife. Terms like profession, or career, or Stay-at Home, seem to be preferential. Perhaps if you associate a dollar value with staying at home as a career and choice, it would mean more.

A salary can be calculated. It isn't that impossible. You make a list of the chores, responsibilities and duties and fees charged for performance and there you have it. Our tallies of this exercise came in from anywhere from $50k to $300k.

According to a recent publication by Reuters, LLC, the value of a stay-at-home-Mom would be in the salary range of $130,000 per year. That figure is based on caring for two children of school age for 100 hours a week (broken down into a regular 40-hour shift and an additional 60 hours of overtime each week). Any mother would argue that in a real 168 hour week (7 days a week, 24 hours a day), especially if her children are not yet school age, that she does not have 68 hours a week to herself, even for sleeping. A similar finding was reported in the May 2, 2005 edition of Newsweek magazine. You can research the topic yourself by looking at the salary.com website. Be the voice for Moms. Bring awareness, appreciation and respect to what you are doing, maybe even a dollar amount.

*I take my role as a mother very seriously, but have never really considered it a job...even though it is by far the most difficult position that I have ever held. Having received a lot of feedback from mothers, I know of none that command a salary for staying at home with the children. Let alone monetary compensation for the endless number of errands, loads of laundry, cooking, etc. that come along with the job. It's not that I'm particularly resentful of doing these associated tasks; I just did them without really paying much attention. Having posed the question, there are a lot of mothers, at first glance, out there that feel like their mothering duties are worth less than $50,000 a year if they were to pay somebody else to do them. However, the monetary value of 24/7 childcare alone would be nearly $100,000 per year at a rate of $11.00/hour. When I thought about it realistically, you wouldn't pay an hourly wage, but an annual salary, which would include paid sick and vacation days.*

Think about motherhood as a salaried career. Is being a stay-at-home mother worth a six-figure income? Should there be time for days off, vacation days, and sick days? How would that change life?

A woman had a master's degree and has never used it. Instead of applying her degree-gained skills to the workforce, she and her husband jointly decided that she would stay home and raise the children. Now her children are 6 and 10, she is restless, struggling and searching for something to fulfill her. It could be called a midlife or better yet, a mid-motherhood crisis. She doesn't know what to do with herself all day long now that the children are both in school fulltime. But mostly she declares that she really wants to go out and earn money and get a paycheck. How crushing to hear this, although totally understandable. Wouldn't it be more accurate to say, "I want to do something else with my life now that my children don't demand my attention all day long"? When she tells herself that she wants to go earn a paycheck, how would she feel if she had been paid all those years with a paycheck? What about the nice house that she lives in? Is that not a paycheck of sorts? Did she not contribute to it? What about the car that she drives and the vacations that she goes on? Are those not monetary paybacks? What is it about this stinking paycheck that makes you think that you are worth more or that we have more? Why does it create your self worth?

Baby boomer wives often were given an allowance or a budget for the household spending. They never had the money discussion, but instead, did what they were taught which was to eke out money from 'somewhere' to buy presents and gifts, trinkets, stuff (important to the woman, not to the man) to decorate the home. Also they were taught to not tell Dad, i.e., the husband. Moms and their girlfriends then kept money secrets all the time. Clothes that were bought were hidden and then suddenly appeared. "Don't tell Daddy" was a common instruction. Many women today tell us that they want to get a 'little job' so that they can have their own spending money. It is part of the 'his money is our money and my money is my money' syndrome. Partly this system get puts into play because the lesser job earner does not make enough money to make a difference so it becomes her personal play money. All of the scenarios above create havoc and inequality. It makes the woman feel like the little girl and the husband becomes the dad whether he intends to be in this role or not. Having to ask your spouse for money is one sure way of creating resentment and hostility. No adult likes to answer to another adult.

*When we decided to get married, we were both working and commanding good salaries. Having both been through divorces, we decided to keep our accounts separate- and we had a discussion about what each of us would be responsible for payment-wise. I think that the decision to keep our accounts separate initially was an attempt to maintain some autonomy, some individual spending power and separate identities.*

*Now that I have scaled way back professionally and we have two children, we re-visited the joint account issue. The transition was not an easy one and we still both have our individual checking accounts, but we now are the proud owners of a joint account.*

*This decision was spurred on by the fact that my money and savings were quickly dwindling and yet I was still paying for a large portion of the* groceries and the kids clothing. We are still working out some of the kinks, but I don't feel like I have to ask my spouse for money anymore. I hated to ask for money because it made me feel like I didn't have an equal say, couldn't spend money freely, and had to watch every cent that I spent. I am not used to playing (or paying) by these rules and have had a difficult time trying to express my needs to my husband. I'm sure that he doesn't mind being the primary breadwinner, or paying for the necessities, because by being home when he's not, I'm actually facilitating his career. Like he has said on many occasions, he couldn't do what he's doing if I weren't doing what I'm doing.

My husband and I don't have similar spending habits. I'm a saver and he's a spender. One of my biggest fears is not making ends meet at the end of the month. I'm much more willing to forego some of the things that I consider self-indulgent like manicures, new clothing, the latest, greatest piece of technology, and even massages, than my spouse is. My husband's spending is quite the opposite. He likes nice new things and does not postpone gratification.

We have had some joint counseling on the financial issues and we see money and debt very differently. This is a fact that is very obvious and not insurmountable, it just takes some effective communication and a willingness to give on both parts. Growing up, I learned that you use credit cards as a means of establishing credit, but that you should not charge anything that you didn't have the cash in the bank to pay for when the statement came due. Although I do like to have nice things, I learned that you should save for them, budget for them, and if you just couldn't make it work, do without until you could. My husband doesn't believe that you have to pay your balance off in full every month. Here we have a sticking point. Even to this day, he thinks that it's ridiculous that I pay my credit card balances off every month, and I think it's crazy to pay a high interest rate your credit card balances. In a sense, we're both right. It's not mandatory to pay off a balance in full every month, but I like the sense of security of knowing that I can pay my bills comfortably every month and knowing that I have all my available credit every month, just in case I need it.

My husband has learned that debt is a necessary evil, and it doesn't really bother him to pay minimum balances in order to ensure adequate cash flow through his business. While I agree with him in theory, I have a *really hard time going against what is prudent as far as my credit cards are concerned, and have never been in debt trouble as a result.*

It is easy to see why this couple has money conflict. Understanding their basic philosophical differences in either postponing gratification or not, allows them to respect one another and not insist on who is right or who is wrong. They are different and need to accommodate for the difference.

There was also a situation where the woman commanded a six-figure income and the man, who had never developed his career, became the Stay-at-Home Dad. When the woman decided that it was time to change the roles, she came home and he went out into Corporate America. He was only able to start off in the high $40s. It was clear that it was going to take some time to work his way up the pay scale and so the only obvious answer was to severely cut back their life style. This created extreme tension in the family because the woman, who was used to getting what she wanted when she wanted it, was financially cut off from most all luxuries, including housekeeper, trips, buying gifts. She shared that even when she was the primary breadwinner she would often ask him if it were okay to buy something. They both agreed that her money was their money. But when she stopped working and bringing in the bacon, she felt like she didn't have any money. His money did not feel like her money. He ironically did not share those feelings of not having money or choices about money when he was the Stay-at-Home Dad. She was completely torn and saw no resolution. She wanted to be home now because there were two babies and she felt like she just couldn't do it all, work full time and have two children at home, even though he was a great Stay-at-Home Dad. And while he was great at being the dad -- grocery shopping, cooking, cleaning up, housekeeping, clothes washing, and ironing were not his forte. It created a very disorganized chaotic household, which was difficult to face after a long day at the office. This couple needed to not only have the tough discussion about money but also the job description that goes along with staying at home.

It was also possible that her staying home full time was much too limited and restrictive. She was definitely good at making money. He was not her equal in that department. They decided through much discussion and professional intervention that the best scenario for them was to each work part time and share the child rearing and household chores.

Money is one of the most difficult topics to be discussed in relationships because of all the emotional baggage that is carried. Spenders marry hoarders and hoarders find the spenders to be their life partners. The surveys showed that many couples do not discuss the nuances of money, as it pertained to everyday circumstances. If you as a Mom no longer 'work' and no longer receive a paycheck, how do you get a pedicure, buy new clothes, and buy presents for your friends and family? Do you have to ask the breadwinner? Are you restricted to a budget? Is he? Do you now feel financially trapped and restricted making money decisions? Did you give up your vote when you gave up your paycheck?

Overwhelmingly Moms who don't work outside the home and who no longer receive a paycheck feel they don't have money. "I don't have any money" is plain and simple faulty thinking. Of course you do. Just because you do not receive a paycheck does not mean you do not have money. It is like the bartering system except that it doesn't look that way. Your ability to create money, advance your career, and grow a business is bartered for creating a home, advancing a family and growing a family.

Have the tough discussion with your husband about money. It's a must. As mentioned before, a budget for the household, just like any corporation should be a mutually agreed upon with the partners it impacts. Never should you feel imprisoned, less than, controlled or like you have to ask 'Daddy' for some money. Never should you be sneaking away money into a cookie jar, so that your husband doesn't know. Of course, the money scene will change and the two of you will have to make adjustments and maybe cut back a little or even a lot when it comes to extras. That part is okay as long as it feels mutual. It will not feel mutual, if he goes and plays golf and has a few drinks with the guys to unwind and you do not have the same privilege because you are no longer bringing in a paycheck! This arrangement will only cause resentment. Resentment creates withhold in love, withhold in the bedroom, withhold with affection, and withhold of liking your partner. Beware of any resentment any time. It is a cancer of all relationships. That is why you need to know how the money is going to work. You need to remain equal in your power and voting power. If one of you works and the other stays home to care for a child, the paycheck belongs to both of you. His money is your money by virtue of staying home. There is no other choice than OUR MONEY. Work out the financial equality piece and life will run much smoother. But HOW, you may ask. Begin by saying, "I really need to know how the money is going to work, if I stay home with the baby." Ask the questions you want answered. If need be, find a qualified therapist, coach, mediator, facilitator, to help you.

*I now realize that being a Mom is a significant role and if I work in addition to that, it's like having a full time 24/7 occupation and squeezing in a part-time job on the side. I do think that my job raising my kids is as important as my spouse's, but it's difficult to overcome the feeling that I couldn't pay the bills with it.*

*I am finally beginning to understand the value that I bring to the family, regardless of the fact that my bank account is not increasing by six-figures annually. I do take my job as a Mom seriously, how could you not? Now I just have to figure out how to work in those vacation days!*

Notice that the above scenario mentioned 'my' bank account, 'my' money. Herein lies some of the challenge. When many women work, it is *their* money in *their* bank account. His is his and Hers is hers. While this is okay when there are no children involved, it is not a workable concept with children and a home. While it is healthy to have ten to twenty percent his and her discretionary money, it creates problems when it feels, looks and is all his money because he is the primary breadwinner and bringing home the paycheck.

If you, the woman, or better yet, the two of you (husband and wife), choose you to be the one who is the primary childcare provider, then you are your partner's financial equal. Whatever the primary breadwinner's paycheck is, you have also earned the income one way or another. First of all, if he gives up his career that begins at $100k and stays out of the job force for even three years, he has lost his competitive edge, which has a price, attached to it. This is called career opportunity loss, which you the woman will experience if you had a career and walk away.

For sake of argument, what if this is correct? What if it is true that you are your partner's financial equal? If you are and you both understand this, then you no longer have to feel less than. Feeling less than plays havoc with your self-esteem, not to mention your attitude, and your secret burning desire to go and get a little job so that you can have some spending money. Bad idea. You already have a job and you already have spending money. Don't financially hijack yourself.

*We are working on meeting in the middle to a certain extent, and this will facilitate our financial future. We both agree that it's important for us to save money so that each of our children can go to college, and we agree that a retirement account is a good idea, and have been saving accordingly. I think over time, we will be on the same financial page- at least that's what I hope.*

*We are only now having the tough financial discussions that we probably should have had before we got married, and certainly before we had a child...let alone two. But overall I think that we are similar enough, and value our relationship enough, that we will find common ground.*

What will it take for you to understand, step up to the plate and command that you are equal to your spouse? Firmly believe that the one that stays home and raises the children is equal in power, money and position. Your voting privileges, your opinions, and your decision-making abilities should not be sacrificed if you sacrifice a career. Given that belief, it may make it easier to decide how to juggle climbing the career ladder or rocking the cradle. Being a breadwinner or breadmaker. Being the Hunter or Gatherer.

This is not the job of your husband. This is your job, your responsibility, your honor and your gift to the generations that follow.

# ~ 10 ~

## Sexy Mama
### *Where Oh Where Did My Libido Go?*

*A*s a new mother, your sexuality can evaporate before your very eyes. After nursing a baby every two hours and literally having someone suck on you those first six months can kill a libido, not to mention physically drain you of energy. The extra pounds of baby fat that takes longer and longer to lose after each child does not help you feel sexy. As Judith Warner stated in her Newsweek Article entitled *Mommy Madness*, some of the mothers that she interviewed and knew were, "...so depleted by the affection and care they lavished upon their small children that they had no energy left, not just for sex, but for feeling like a sexual being." This puts not only a strain on you but on your spouse as well. Is he supposed to just wait patiently? Well, yes. Wouldn't that be nice? And, is he supposed to surprise you with flowers for no reason? Wouldn't that be even nicer? Is he supposed to through osmosis know just the right thing to say and more importantly the right thing NOT to say? Well, of course. If only this were possible! And the real truth is that he probably is really good at saying all the wrong things at all the wrong times and is helplessly impatient because he doesn't understand. No one has given him the instruction manual, which will be your job. Not another job you cry! Yes, sorry, you need to tell him exactly what you want and don't want and more importantly not take his clumsiness and ineptitude personally.

Couples need to know that their sex lives will change. It will probably go away for a while in the sense that a pregnant body often doesn't feel sexy. Then there is the time after the anxiously awaited six-week check up following the baby's birth. Most men are counting the days until that moment, and most women are still thinking and/or saying 'keep that thing AWAY from me'! The disparity in sexual desire at six weeks after having a baby could probably go down in history as the greatest moment of disparity. Usually if you do not get your pre-baby figure back quickly, feeling sexy is difficult. Your clothes are still tight, or you may even be in your pregnancy clothes. Rarely do your once tight jeans that you proudly strutted around in, and your cute short-cropped top that flashed a tight belly fit after six weeks, let alone six months.

It is interesting how after having a baby (and directly within the first year or so), your husband's sexuality and desire start feeling like 'just one more thing you have to do and you have to give'. Somewhere during the course of pregnancy, giving birth and being a new mother, you can easily forget that you once enjoyed sex. Making love was satisfying and mutual. Being sexual was a lovely escape for you as well. Perhaps it is just the experience of having a baby literally depend on your body to live that burns out your own body's desire to be touched. Many women say that they avoid kissing their husbands romantically because it will be interpreted by them that they want sex, so if you don't start the kiss, it won't go there. French kissing or even kissing before you had a baby could have just been fun foreplay and fooling around, now it is weighted. This is a tough discussion to have. However, it is an important discussion to have. It sounds like this, 'Honey, if I kiss you, it doesn't always mean that I want to have sex. The reason I don't kiss you anymore is because I don't want to feel the pressure of having to have sex.' 'Or right now, I would just like to be held. Help me not have your hugs and your caresses feel like pressure.' Without this tough discussion, a silent wedge between you and your partner can insidiously grow and grow. Without conversation around this topic, you are each left to your own interpretation of what is going on, what changed and why. He can easily feel disregarded and not loved, and may make comments that imply that there is something wrong with you. You can feel alone, not understood and imperfect.

What about the couple or the mother that decides that she wants to raise her baby via the attachment theory, a part of which is responding as immediately as possible to the child's every need? It is also a parenting style that advocates co-sleeping with the child in the bed with Mom and Dad. One such couple's child slept in their bed until he was six years old. And while this may be extreme and unusual, how do you feel about the baby in bed with you? How does your husband feel? Guess who quickly becomes the odd man out…literally. The husband. Is it any wonder that jealousy or resentment could begin to brew? And even though you are supposed to be mature adults, the husband could easily feel replaced, displaced and not at the top of your world. This is hard on men. Men like to be the center of a woman's universe. …and many were/are until the baby arrives. Then boom, baby comes along and he is kicked off the pedestal. Sex and lovemaking can get lost in all of this change.

Talking about these issues and having the difficult conversations can ease the transition. Conversely, if handled tenderly, the woman can see her man as her man and not as her little boy. But if you become 110% Mom, then your eyes become blind to anything but Daddy when you look at your spouse. Do you want to know how to ruin a perfectly great lover relationship? You become the controlling mother (in and out of bed) and he will easily fall into the role of pouting little boy. Then you reverse roles. He becomes the controlling father (with the money and your life) and you become the pouting little girl. How many couples do you see fall into this? Is it really so basic that because he wants sex and you won't give it to him, that he sees that you want money and he won't dole it out…unless he gets sex? Does that really happen? And if you give him sex, will he give you money? Do financial issues really spill into the bedroom…or is it the other way around? Do bedroom 'issues' i.e., lovemaking or the lack thereof, really dictate and drive the bank account? What is wrong with this picture? How did it all turn into a power struggle? Who is controlling whom? What happened to equality?

Sometimes couples do all of the above and have no idea what is going on or why there is so much tension and withhold. Numerous couples with relationship difficulties, have been asked, 'when did you start having difficulties in your relationship?' They almost always say, right after our first son or daughter was born. This can go back 5, 10, 20 years! Everything changed then. And they are right. Everything does change when you bring a baby into the world. When people are in therapy and they are struggling with their relationship and they want to have a baby, the prognosis is not good. It is the surest path to ruin an already fragile relationship. Babies don't really bond people and make their love for one another grow. Babies can do this for certain, but never is it recommended to risk having a baby so that the relationship gets better. If it is bad before the baby, it's very likely to be worse afterwards.

Every new parent (Moms and Dads alike) will attest to the fact that your sex life changes. For Moms, you simply do not have time, energy, or spontaneity at your disposal as you once did. For Dads, spontaneity has gone bye-bye, and surely time has been shortened. Dads' energy and desire for sex has not necessarily changed, or if it has, it has probably increased. Once you both accept the facts and the differences, there will need to be some tough discussions around how do you keep the romance alive in your relationship.

Don't let the latest how to revive your sex life articles discourage you or make you feel even worse than you already do because they appear to present you with some magical formula. You need to have the discussion with your husband about what you need and what he needs and work on a plan that works for both of you. Don't feel bad because you're not up for having sex 25 times a month. Who needs the gold stars? And who is counting anyway? Well, he may be counting, but try focusing on quality and let go of quantity.

Becoming parents, bringing a child into the work is serious business challenging and testing the deepest parts of you. Sex and money will be the elephants in the room. The willingness to take and make the time to have the tough discussions around money and sex will be excellent eye-openers for challenging and stimulating communication of what to expect and how to resolve and avoid resentment. Again, get professional help with this if necessary. As crass and unromantic as it may sound, sex and money become pawns in a chess game only creating winners and losers if the rules are not clearly and openly defined. A golden nugget of truth: hanging on to your passion and romance for one another goes hand in hand with staying each other's financial equal. Sound odd? Check it out. Resolving sex and money issues could make the difference between a ho-hum marriage and an extraordinary journey into a dynamic alive empowered relationship.

# ~ 11 ~

## Have the Tough Discussions

Tough discussions are tough. That is why you usually take the path of least resistance and avoid the conversation. It's not fun, it's not easy, and it certainly isn't comfortable to talk about things that are touchy subjects--sex and money ranking right at the top. However, if you don't have the tough discussions, feelings of resentment fester, grow and usually spill out in hurtful and harmful ways such as little digs and jabs, zingers in front of company. If you are feeling resentful for any reason, this resentment will eat up your relationship like a slow growing cancer. Get outside professional help if need be. Make it a policy that if something is bugging you, you have a way to get it out in the open and on the table. Choosing to avoid the tough discussions may be easier in the short run, and it may be what you have done your whole life, but it is never without a price-and a very steep price at that. In the end it could cost you your relationship.

# ~ 12 ~

# Cut Him Some Slack
## He's a Man!

$\mathcal{A}$s mentioned earlier in the book, mothers hear their babies cry in the night and Dads are notorious for somehow sleeping through the wails. It is easy to jump to the conclusion that women are just more in tuned with their child. Well, duh. How could you not be? You just carried a life from embryo to gestation in your very own body. It can even feel like women 'care' more, and that Moms love more. Men annoy women with their ability to sleep through the night, their ability to not think of every detail and circumstance that might come up, and not pre-determine everything that the baby will need. Women can really make this a personal matter and become miffed quite easily. You can count on your husband to say the wrong thing. It may begin as early as the day you found out that you're pregnant. It is really a 50/50 chance that he will say just the right thing that you want to hear. It is common knowledge that many times the husband is not as excited as the wife expects he should be. He does not get excited about the baby moving, doesn't seem sympathetic when a miscarriage occurs and doesn't seem nearly as touched as the Mom when he gazes at his new baby. Your hormones are raging, and more often than not, it's your hormones responding to the things that your husband says. Hormonally challenged? Yes, you are. Being hypersensitive goes with the territory and probably anything he says can hurt your feelings.

Motherhood and fatherhood do not look equal on the outside. The experience is different. You may feel that you are getting the short end of the stick, but he may feel that too in his own way. If God had determined that men were to be the mothers and give birth, the whole experience would probably be government subsidized. Men by socialization and nature would never allow doormat behavior. They would have formed fraternities and Rotary Clubs around fatherhood and the woes and tolls taken.

Fathers usually hang on to their careers and status and add "Dad" to their repertoire of titles. Fathering, referring to the chores and tasks of the title, is something that they can do after work and on the weekends. In fact, many of our Moms reported in the survey that to them their husbands' lives didn't appear to change all that much. From a woman's perspective it looks like, in general, men get to compartmentalize their work and their titles. What women see is that what men let go of is probably golf games (well not as many), drinking beer with their buddies and all that other 'guy stuff' that they put in balance with being the new parent. Many Dads would protest that it is not that cut and dried. Both women and men agree that what they take on is an enormous sense of responsibility and pressure to make high financial goals. And yet with that being said, why is this scenario so common? He says, 'Honey, I only work hard for you and the kids. She says, "I don't care about being a multi-millionaire…. That is not my goal!' He retorts back, "Yeah right, she doesn't care about the big house, housekeeper, the trips, the presents, the private schools…on and on and on!" Off and running they go. Once again, man not hearing woman, woman not hearing man.

Men tackle life differently and more linearly. They tend to want to pinpoint the problem and quickly find the solution. Period. A man could easily deduce when the baby is born that because he is no longer the priority, the baby takes over naturally, that he is less important. Problem: "I'm not the Top Dog at home anymore." Solution: "Go where I am important. Take charge of what I have control over. Making money. I know how to do that."

A full time stay-at-home Mom noticed that after the first three months her husband worked later and later each night. It seemed that he had to travel more as well. Work became extremely demanding and kept creating pressure and opportunities that took him away from home more and more often. Life has a way of doing this, creating all or nothing. But there was more to the story than the age-old argument of 'Honey, I am working hard to give you and the kids all the luxuries in life! You certainly like the nice house and the nice car and the ability to buy whatever you want. Cut me some slack!' The truth was revealed years later as he admitted that he felt completely and totally unimportant and dethroned in her world. He found comfort not in the arms of his wife, who was usually holding a baby, but in the comfort of making his fortune and rising to the CEO of the company.

Men, new Dads among the top of the list, report feeling used, not valued and not a priority in their woman's life. Like their women counterparts, they too start keeping score, either consciously or subconsciously and the cold war begins. Men, also report that they do not feel understood and frustrated that whatever they try, and as many times as they attempt to fix the problem, they meet with failure. For the man who like to fix things and is usually a success at work because this is what he is good at...problem solving.... all that is left to do is to emotionally go away.

Therefore, give him an instruction manual. Tell him what you want. Tell him how to say it, how to do it and how to show up. Cut him some slack. He is a man, not a woman. He is having a father experience not a mother one. And he can only be the father. By the way, women have no idea what it feels like to be a Dad. Many dear well-intended men try to show up, only to fail time after time again. You be the Mom and let him be the Dad. Sound obvious? It may be that Moms are a pushy bunch, especially if they are 'captaining the ship.' Mom may need to be reminded that she really only has to be the Mom. Learning to constantly mother your children and remind them to brush their teeth, etc, often becomes such a way of being that we begin to treat our spouse like another child. Bad idea. Very, very bad idea.

So when you are doing your own thing, or taking time for yourself, or going to a class and Dad is home alone with the children, it is a good thing. It is good for Dad to be in charge without you around. It is good for the children to have just Daddy. Let him do things his way when he is in charge. Give him some space. Let him come around in his own time, his own way. There is plenty of time for him to be more involved than you...and it has nothing to do with you or with his love for his baby. Let him do the best he can. Give him time. Give him alone time and opportunity to become the Dad he is capable of being.

## On Women

Helen Fisher writes, "...Women tend to gather more data that pertain to a topic and connect these details faster. Women integrate, generalize, and synthesize." She calls this web thinking. "Ancestral women had the hardest job of any creature that ever trod the earth; raising long dependent babies under highly dangerous conditions. In order to rear helpless infants, ancestral mothers needed to do a lot of things at the same time. Watch for snakes. Listen for thunder. Taste for poison. Rock the sleepy. Distract the cranky. Instruct the curious. Soothe the fearful. Inspire the tardy. Feed the hungry. Mothers had to do countless daily chores while they stoked the fire, cooked the food and talked to friends."

## On Men

Helen Fisher also writes, "As a general rule, men tend to focus on one thing at a time. Men are good at compartmentalizing their attention. Their thinking process is, on average, more channeled. Faced with a business problem, men tend to focus on the immediate dilemma rather than putting this issue in a larger context. They progress in a straightforward, linear, causal path toward a specific goal: the solution. They like to weed out what appears to be extraneous, unrelated data to focus on the task at hand." She calls this focused, compartmentalizing, and incremental reasoning process; step thinking.

"A million years ago ancestral men were building fires, chipping stone hand axes, and hunting big animals in East Africa. As they pursued these dangerous beasts, men had to concentrate, peering from behind a bush, crouching near a water hole, slipping past a sleeping leopard in a tree, trailing cantankerous wounded creatures, then attacking when the time was right.

Those who didn't pay strict attention were gored, trampled or eaten. So as our male forebears tracked warthogs and wildebeests, they gradually evolved the brain architecture to screen out peripheral thoughts, focus their attention and make step-by-step decisions."

Doesn't it help to understand and buy into the fact that it is in our DNA? Moms are multi-taskers because they are wired this way! Dads are single focused because they are wired that way! It doesn't really mean that women care more about their young than men do! It doesn't really mean Dads only care about themselves, their money, their golf game, and their cars. They can turn off the family because the family is not in front of them 24/7. It is probably rare that men go to work and while they are at work, they wish they were at home. And when they are at home, they wish they were at work…. Well, maybe. Women are process oriented. They are gatherers and gathering…. all possibilities…all of the time.

This is why women bring up all the extraneous details of a situation. For example, when questioned by her husband with 'What's wrong Honey?' She replies, "I can't do it all! I can't change the baby, set the table, make dinner, do the dishes, give them baths, read a story, put the pajamas on, and then want to jump into bed and make passionate love to YOU!"

What did I do, he ponders! When he asks what is wrong, he might as well be saying what is broken? How can I fix it? What is the problem? Tell me, I can fix it! Well as you all know by now, you don't want to be fixed. You usually don't want a solution. What you want is to be heard! Women want to vent, be heard and be validated. Magic answer: 'Wow, Honey, it sounds really exhausting to be a Mom and then to make matters worse, to think that you have to do something for me, too!" It is not what men do as much as what they don't see to do, and they certainly don't say the right thing at the right time. The miscommunication goes round and round.

Men don't want to linger in the process. They are hunters, hunting, focusing on the solution at hand. Find the solution to the problem so that this (this being the emotional outpour of feelings and stress) will go away and I can get onto the next step. He may even make up a problem, just to be able to give some order to the chaos i.e., tears, sobs, raging hormones, and to be helpful. Again single focus, he wants to find the solution to what he thinks is the problem. He really has no idea what the real problem is, but he will fix it just the same. In pure frustration he blurts out, "I told you to keep the Nanny longer if you want". She doesn't want the Nanny longer; she wants him to GET IT! GET IT is translated into prove to me that you really understand what a hard frustrating and unrewarding day I just had!

Men don't get it. More importantly however, women don't get that men don't get it. And they never will. They are different. Women lament this situation all of the time over and over and over. Women keep insisting and fighting with men to just simply get it! This is impossible. Get it? Get that it is impossible for a man to think and act like a woman.

*"Each sex is playing with a different deck of evolutionary cards."*

*Helen Fisher*

He doesn't really get what it is like to be pregnant and he certainly can't relate to being sucked on all day and all night as you nurse your precious little one. He doesn't get it-because he can't. He is not a woman and try as he may, he will probably not be as good of a listener to the late night feeding sagas as your girlfriend is that just went through the same experience and who can even finish your sentences for you! And more often than not, he doesn't hear the baby cry in the middle of the night. He probably slept right through it. Please stop making him wrong for this.

Newborns are intimidating. If it is scary for you, even though you have the instincts and have carried the child, it could be sheer terror for him. Cut him some slack on how he burps the baby and how he carries the baby (it often resembles carrying a football). Let him change the diaper his way (and make sure you get out of the way so that he has the opportunity). And if he takes the baby out and forgets the diaper bag, but sticks a bottle in one pocket and a diaper in the other, only smile and keep your mouth shut. And don't forget to say Gee, you're a great Dad and turn your head and go the other way.

Many Dads back off because they can become incredibly intimidated. They take the low man on the totem pole position because they quickly become and feel like the low man on the totem pole. Mothers by nature are such controlling, in charge creatures when it comes to tending their young. They quickly become the experts even when they are not.

Take the next story, for example:

*I am reminded of my own first experience when the father turned to me and asked me how to change a diaper. I had no clue, had no younger siblings, never baby-sat and literally had no idea. But after I burst into tears, I acted like I did, made it up and then was there to make sure and point out if the diaper was on wrong or not. My excuse is that I was very, very young. I didn't know (and this was 34 years ago and in a time before disposable diapers) that diapers could go on in a variety of ways provided that the essentials were covered, and the most important thing is that both Mom and Dad learn to change a diaper in their own way. This was the time before equality was spelled out as it is today. To shock you young mothers even more, I never considered 'sharing' changing the diapers or taking turns getting up in the night. I thought he had every right to pick and choose what he wanted to do and how he wanted to show up as Daddy.*

Many men experience their own emotional overwhelm when they are a Dad and a Provider. They are now adults that cannot (nor should not) quit a job on a whim and travel to Europe with a backpack for six months. This enormous sense of responsibility plays out in every facet of the married couple's life. Men do change when they become fathers. Some remark that they really don't want to play golf after work, or go to the bars, or stay at the gym. They want to come home and see their little ones. Some experience a total inner contentment and often marvel at their choice. Likewise, their circle of friends changes. Just as their single buddies changed into married buddies, the circle of friends slowly evolves into hanging out with other Dads because there is simply more in common. This isn't a case for who has it worse or who has it better. This is not a contest. It is simply different.

# ~ 13 ~

## Cut Yourself Some Slack
### You're a Woman!

There is no way to know beforehand the enormous challenge being a mother creates. It is more profound for the woman than the man, since in most instances the woman is the one that is the primary care taker. Being the primary caretaker puts you in the position of deciding how to continue your career. Should you work outside of the home for income or choose to Stay-at-Home and be the full time caregiver? No matter what you choose, you still end up being emotionally and physically responsible for the baby. It still leaves you, Mom, finding the nanny, checking out the babysitter, giving the instructions, and micro-managing childcare. The harsh reality is, even if you are not tending the baby, you are still is in charge of who is.

So much happens to you on every measurable facet of your being. The first and most obvious is your physical body and the changes that it goes through and continues to go through-particularly if breast-feeding. Losing the 'baby fat' has it own set of stressors. Especially if you are nursing, you cannot starve yourself and lose weight overnight.

Nursing requires that you put so many calories into your body. Make sure that you cut yourself some slack and do not expect to be back to your size 6 pants until it is reasonable to be there. And yes, at some point return to your pre baby weight. It feels wonderful.

There is also the issue of exercising. It will take not only time to feel like exercising, but then it will take organizing someone to watch the baby, working around feeding schedules. The desire to go to the gym if you have been up and awake every two hours feeding the newborn presents its own challenge. Realize that you don't have to go to the gym, do whatever type of exercise that you have time and energy to do. Make exercise a simple and enjoyable part of your day. For example, it could be as simple as taking your dog, your child in a stroller, or both for a walk in the evening. The point here is to be nice to you. Listen to what your body needs, not what your pride, ego, and image tell you to do. Your body may tell you to take a nap or chill out. Work on your perfect body weight later, after you get some other things under control.

Women 25-40 years old have been raised in an environment to want to do it all, have it all, and be it all, all at once. It ain't gonna happen. Relax, slow down, and enjoy the ride. As all women say, these first 3 years go so fast and yet at the time feel so profoundly tediously slow. Children really do grow up. Anyone with school age children may only dimly remember those sleepless nights, those long repetitive days of nursing, changing a diaper, doing another load of laundry and then doing it all over again and again and again in what at the time seems like an endless process. How can that be? How can something totally absorb and transform your life, every fiber in your body, and then you forget about it?

It gets easier, promise. You may never forget all of the chores, sleepless nights, or loads of laundry, but the tedium pales over time. If you ever need some reassurance that what you're doing is important and worthwhile, spend a few minutes watching and listening to your children when they are playing solo. You'll be smiling in no time, guaranteed.

# ~ 14 ~

## Delegate, Share, Ask For Help

All too often mothers refuse to allow people to help them, thinking that they should be able to do it all themselves. After all, Generation X mothers have been, "...bred to be independent and self-sufficient" (Warner, Newsweek). One of the questions on the survey asked was do you actually use your support network or do you think that you should be able to do it all yourself? Surprisingly, only about 50% of our interviewees reported having a support network that they could rely on to help them with their children, and of those that had a support network, more than 90% of these women felt guilty asking for help.

A CEO of a major company does not do every single job by herself; she hires competent people to help her. A Stay-at-Home CEO may not have the financial resources to hire out childcare, but there are other ways to ensure that you are not expecting the impossible of yourself. Use your support network. Ask your family to help you out once in a while. Investigate a babysitting co-op arrangement with your Mom friends. Many articles have been written on this subject of support and support groups for Moms. Give yourself permission to not only let someone (responsible) take care of your children once in awhile, but to be creative about it as well.

In addition to figuring out ways to share the child-care load, consider hiring a housekeeper. Having a housekeeper for a Mom is like having a caddie on the golf course. Of course you could carry your own clubs, but having a caddie is a huge treat! Having someone else clean the toilets, scrub the shower, sparkle up the stove, refrigerator and countertops is downright heaven. Any amount of time will be a tremendous help, and it's as good (and decadent) as chocolate! Please tell me why not? No money you say, are you sure? Does the family not spend this in lattes, dinners out, and impulse buys? $40/week should give you 2-4 hrs of housekeeping. $40 times 4 equals $160/month...are you sure? Can you really say that? Isn't it easy to piddle away less than $6/ a day? That can happen every time you go to the grocery store.

# ~ 15 ~

## Hang On To Yourself

$\mathcal{B}$e true to yourself. What does this mean? It means that you need to take a little time and energy and do some introspection. It is your job to determine what works for you as a person, a mother, and you and your husband as a team. You don't have to subscribe to a particular method, style, ideal or image; but you need to sift through the current literature and plethora of parenting advice and take what you like out of it, and simply discard the rest.

*I was going to be the perfect mother, have children that slept through the night, napped on schedule and allowed me to have some time for myself. What I found was that one of my children was eager to please and receive praise and external validation, and the other could care less about what anyone else thought about what she was doing. The methods that I used successfully to get my first child to sleep were not successful with my second. Although I tried with both to get them to take the bottle (of formula, no less) so that I could share the feeding experience with my husband, neither of my children took it willingly, and after a while, I gave up. What I was trying to do was make my children conform to the advice that I had read*

*in the various parenting books. What I wasn't doing was listening to my
intuition or my children. It wasn't long before I decided that I wasn't
going to force my children to do anything. I began to trust my instinct and
intuition and with that shift, everyone was a lot happier.*

Remember that there is no magic cookie-cutter recipe for parenting
your particular children. You don't have to conform to any set of
ideas. Experiment, test, and figure out what works best for you and
your family. If you're having any doubts about whether something is
working, trust that your children will let you know. Also know that
what worked for one child may not work for the other. Be flexible, be
creative, and find the best way for both you and your child. If some
method is working, stick with it until it doesn't work any longer. Don't
hang on to it if you are beating your head against the wall. The delicate
balance is knowing when you, the parent, need to make the decision
and your child is resisting. You are the CEO after all! Children do
know some things that they need. However bedtime is not a child's
decision. You need to be the parent and make parental decisions and
set boundaries. Be creative in how you get there.

It is okay to ask for or pay for help with the children. A nanny,
an au pair, a girlfriend, your sister, your parents....use them! Trading
one morning a week with another Mom, you watch her kids and she
watches yours, is a grand idea. Start out small. An hour, then two,
then a whole morning, a whole day....wow, maybe even overnight!

Does any CEO run the entire company by him or herself? Honestly.
Doesn't every successful person have some help some of the time?
Success is built around synergy, teams, and delegation. Of course, you
may think you can do it all. But why? And at what expense? Does it
maximize your efficiency? Does it really increase the bottom line...on
the home front? An exhausted, unhappy, depressed, haggard Mom is
not the goal. And why? No one will thank you and no one will help
you with this but you.

Be something other than a Mommy. Be a writer, an artist, a
draftsman, a photographer, or a consultant. A few hours a week will
create some balance for you. Hold onto at least a part of your 'adult'
self. An absolute must. Mommy is a totally consuming all absorbing
role. Stepping out of it periodically, some time each day, really creates

powerful results. It allows you to not lose your self in this long journey.

Yoga classes, Pilates, take something somewhere where you can be something other than someone's Mom. It gives you sanity. Listen to this mother's story:

_For me, it began as becoming a Transcendental Meditator. I 'stole' 20 minutes a day, once at 5 am and again at 5pm and meditated. My young children finally got used to it and used to say, "shhhhh she's meditaping!!! Then it turned to exercise. I became a tennis player, then a runner. After my two hours of playing tennis, I always was a better Mom. Everyone was just fine with Mom doing something for herself, once Mom was fine with it first._

After the first six weeks and being worried about not exercising, know that exercise is an absolute must. Exercise of any sort will do. 30-60 min of exercise 5 days a week however it is easiest for you. Make sure that you schedule yourself time to get your exercise in, and make sure it's something that you enjoy doing. Pilates, yoga, spin class, weights, running, walking, and swimming.... Anything, break a sweat! Non-negotiable. Top-level CEO's use the very same criteria. It is called stress management. It is called pacing yourself. It is called balance so that you can last longer and not come on with a bang and end with a burn.

Cut yourself some slack if you start to feel boring, stodgy, and find yourself humming 'the wheels on the bus go round and round, round and round, round and round' even when you are alone. Sometimes you might cry because your pretty blouse just got throw-up on it for the second time. You will definitely crave adult conversation with anyone who will listen. This is all normal. This goes with the territory. This also is temporary. Promise.

Cut yourself some slack if you truly want to go back to work, get out of the house and you do not want to be a full time Stay-at-Home Mom. Some women are just not cut out for it.

_I don't think that women should have to stay at home if they don't find it satisfying, but I certainly don't think that women who stay at home should feel like losers. As I have said before, staying at home with children, in my experience is infinitely more stressful than working at the office. I'm_ *not sure why, but it is. What I wish for myself, is that whatever I choose to do, I feel proud…not guilty, not ashamed, not stressed about the decision. I'm working on getting to that point. I know that for me personally, keeping even the tiniest toehold in the adult world is necessary. I like to have adult conversations, interact with adults other than my spouse and friends, and have a little mental challenge. I am a work-at-home mother, and I think that my kids are better off for it. If I am able to spend just a little bit of time writing, working, whatever while someone else plays with my kids, I'm a much better Mom at the end of the day, and to me, that's what it's all about. And as I think this, I wish this for ALL moms across the globe to have peace with their choice.*

*I recently had a maternal epiphany. I was thinking about my career and my family and it dawned on me that in my career at my job, I spent each and every day in an expendable position working hard for clients who really didn't matter that much to me in the long run. As a mother, at home, I am working harder than ever at the essential position of raising my children. I am not expendable as a mother or wife, and right now my energies are focused on working for the people that matter the very most in my life. Since my epiphany, I have been much more at peace with my role in the family and my position as a Mom.*

In conclusion, an exciting career and paycheck are seductive to any woman. And giving up career and paycheck to motherhood conceptually speaking, hits below the belt if you compare money to mommy. Let it be in print that not all women are baby crazy. Not all women feel that instant bond. Many women don't enjoy the baby stage. It's okay. And it isn't just postpartum depression. Some women relate better when they can actually communicate verbally with the child. You do the best that you can. Just be you. Bottom line: being a Mom is the greatest spiritual and heartfelt experience. It can be the worst financial and professional experience. Change this. Make a win/win experience. Do you want it all? Yes, of course because motherhood deserves to be all that it can be.

The good news is that you and your attitude have the power to change the status of motherhood. It begins with you. It begins with you honoring your role and demanding, structuring and creating the dignity that you deserve. So to begin with never again, apologize for being a Stay-at-Home Mom.... or any kind of a Mom for that matter. Say it loudly and say it proudly, even if at first you have to fake it.

"Million Dollar Mommy" is intended to give you the power to turn yourself into a Million Dollar Mom. Feel and live the power of your own path of motherhood. Discover the six secrets to finding pride in your choices and decisions. Empower yourself to be as good as you can be whether you choose to stay in society's workforce, or engage yourself in your own empire at home. Lastly, be at peace, trust and give thanks for the opportunity to have the greatest experience on earth.

# Epilogue

In Helen Fisher's book, *The First Sex The Natural Talents of Women and How They are Changing the World*, she quotes historian Gerda Lerner stating that, "...The huge baby boom generation is reaching middle age. As anthropologists have documented, middle-aged women around the world tend to become much more assertive. With menopause, levels of the estrogens decline, unmasking natural levels of testosterone and other androgens in the female body. Androgens, male sex hormones, are potent chemicals regularly associated with assertiveness and rank in many mammalian species, including people. Such a critical mass of older women with a tradition of rebellion and independence and a way of making a living has not occurred before in history."

If this is true for baby boomer women, imagine the impact that women of the x and y generations will have on society. Baby boomer women are late bloomers when it comes to assertiveness and if they need the menopause thing to kick in, then so be it. There are a lot of feisty 50 and 60-year-old women around. They are not taking middle age lightly or lazily. They are not rushing out to get their AARP cards activated. In fact, there is a huge cry of IT'S MY TURN!!!! Hopefully the next generation has learned to not wait this long to take a turn. Remember baby boomers bred the me, me, me generation. Maybe this is why it is so challenging to have a baby today and to know what exactly to do! Work or not work outside of the home? Maybe the attitude is exactly the reason for feeling emotionally hijacked by motherhood. Maybe you do have a reason to want it all, right now. A great upward moving career, a beautiful balanced family life, a passionate romantic relationship with your husband and time for pedicures and Pilates. Whew! That's a lot. All at once. Right now.

There is time! There is time to go to college. There is time to have a career. There is time to raise your babies. There is time to go back to college. There is time to start another career. There is even time after you retire to do something that you have always wanted to do like open a pizza parlor, write a mystery novel or go study art in Italy for the summer. Your babies will be even more assertive, more self-confident and more full of it than you are!

*When I was a young mother at the tender age of 24, with 3 babies by the time I was 30, I didn't really see life beyond kids. I didn't even see life beyond them all being in school at the same time. It was quite all consuming and devoured my attention and time. My mother's words of they are only little once did nothing but annoy me...easy for her say! And, in fact, she was prophetically correct.*

"On the farm, women needed many children to pick the beans, milk the cows, and collect the eggs. Children were a cheap, reliable essential part of the farm labor force.

New inventions have accelerated the decline in birthrates. So a woman no longer has to conceive several infants in hopes that two or three will live. Thus married women generally have more years to work before getting pregnant. They also remain at work longer during pregnancy, return to work sooner after bearing babies and have fewer pregnancies that interrupt their careers. In fact, today women on average spend less time being pregnant and caring for children than at any time in human evolution," states Helen Fisher in *The First Sex*.

Mothers between 25 and 40, be aware that there is plenty of time and that this particular juncture into motherhood is time limited.

*I know that as a mother of a 34-year-old, 30-year-old and 27 year old, I am still a Mom but I did such a darn good job that they don't need me anymore. Our relationship is purely pleasurable. Oh sure, I am needed for a good home-cooked meal every now and then, but not really needed. I have time to do and to be whatever I want to do and to be. And I am far from sitting in a rocking chair reflecting on the good old days. My point being that if you are so inclined and are able to be a stay at home mom fulltime, my guess is that when your children are grown and on their own, you will not regret it for a minute.*

The choice is yours. Even if you think that you really have to work just to make ends meet. That is still a choice that you are making about where you live, how you live, what you **want** to give your family etc.

You really aren't a victim of the world you see. And if you feel like a victim, you will feel unhappy, trapped and down. Don't be a victim of motherhood. Know that you are going to get emotionally hijacked and understand what this means and how to get unhijacked. Take care of yourself. Enjoy and be proud of being a mom. Love where you land. This too shall pass, all too quickly. Enjoy the ride. Enjoy the journey. Be true to yourself and find the right combination that fits for you.

Mothers are the barometers of the household. Everyone else truly does rotate around the mother's mental, physical and emotional well-being. Pose yourself this question, if money were no object, what would you do?

# The Six Secrets

Here are six secrets that are essential to making a successful transition from full-time career person to Mom:

## 1.   Be The CEO Of The Home

All ships have a captain. All companies have a CEO. All households need a captain, CEO, leader, decision maker, someone in charge. Step up to the plate. Take charge. It will empower you and all those around you. Yes, of course, you can share job titles, tasks and chores. But in the end, Mom is pretty much the barometer of the household. Traditionally this is true and even now with the change of times, women's liberation, equality and affirmative action. In the end when it is all said and done, the woman runs the children scene and the homefront. She always has and probably always will. We want to make it official. We want to speak it aloud. Claim your role and your territory. We know that Motherhood is not a punishment but a reward. It is also a tremendous responsibility. Remember, responsibility means the ability to respond. Respond by being in charge.

## 2.   Create Your Own Personal Perks

No one knows better than you how tired you are, how drained you become and how frustrating it can be being a new Mom. No one knows better than YOU what you need and what you don't need. Take care of yourself so that you can take care of your loved ones. The more you give yourself, the more you will have to give. Be proactive in the process. Schedule down time for yourself. Keep it in check. Give up the drama of waiting until you are sick in bed, pathetic and pale. Bring balance to your work and your play. All will appreciate this in the end. You will be a better Mom, wife and woman.

## 3.     Have The Tough Discussions (Sex and Money)

Sex and Money come up every single day, whether the words are actually spoken or not. However, literally talking about sex and money issues is often avoided and danced around. The attitude is usually that somehow, this 'stuff' will either just go away or get mysteriously solved. The hard truth is that if you don't talk about the problems, they will never get resolved. Resentment will slowly simmer and seethe. And since sex and money are extremely emotionally charged topics, if you are not effective in communicating about these loaded topics, we highly encourage getting professional help. Speak your truth. Be brave and have the tough discussions. Empower yourself financially and sexually. Explain your needs, your interpretations, your assumptions. Listen to his. Try to walk in his shoes and ask him to walk in yours. Find the win/win. Stay away from being the winner, for it only produces a loser.

## 4.     Hang On To Your Self

Before you were a Mom, you were someone else. Before you were a wife, you were something else. You had friends. You had hobbies. You had dreams. You had goals. Do not lose sight of these. Yes, some will have to take a back seat. Some will go away because priorities and interests change. But do not lose the essence of your being. Do not give all of yourself to your children, spouse and the family pet. Stay interested in your passions and you will remain passionate. Keep a toe in the water. Keep the spark alive, don't let your inner fire burn or be put out completely. All will be richer, if you hang onto yourself.

## 5.     Be A Million Dollar Mommy

We are excited and thrilled to offer YOU the option of becoming a Million Dollar Mommy. Grab the challenge by the horns. Be a walking testimony to positive, powerful and peaceful images and beings of motherhood. No generation has ever been more prepared or more positioned to transform motherhood into a beautiful and desirable role model. Be your own version of a Million Dollar Mommy. Claim your worth and put it out there for the world to see and emulate. What a gift to give your children. Change the respect of the role for both sons and daughters of the generation to come. Be worth it, because you are.

## 6.    Trust Yourself To Make The Right Decisions

When you learn to listen to your inner voice, your intuition, your gut feelings, life runs much smoother. Only you, not your husband, mother, mother-in-law, friends or society know what it is that you need to do to be peaceful inside. Some of you need to give up your careers, now or maybe forever. Perhaps that chapter of your life is over or closed for the time being. Some of you need to keep your careers going. The career and all that it entails may be what you are best at and driven to do. If so, do it. Some of you need to do a little bit of both. Whatever the secret combination is you hold the key. Trust yourself to make the right decisions about career, staying home part time, or full time. Trust yourself to be the kind of Mom in your heart that you are and always will be.

Appendix – Motherhood Questionnaire

# Motherhood Questionnaire

*We are basing these questions under the assumption that there are two parents raising the children.*

*To respond to this questionnaire, please type in your answers after each question.*

## Definitions:

*Professional Career/profession* – projects and services completed for compensation by another party. This could be working from home or working outside the home

*Spouse* – any domestic partner/co-parent other than the mother

*Stay-at-Home Mom-* Mom that stays home full time and her primary work is raising her child/children.

*Career Mom-* Mom that works both at home as a stay-at-home mom and has an outside career.

## Demographic Information

1)      Age:
2)      Where do you live?
3)      How old were you when you had your children?
4)      Number of children:
5)      Ages of children:
6)      Current Income Bracket  (state a, b, c, or d):
       a.  $25,000-$50,000
       b.  $50,000-$75,000
       c.  $75,000 - $100,000
       d.  $100,000 +
7)      Is your current income bracket based on one or two incomes?
8)      Income bracket before children (state a, b, c, or d):
       a.  $25,000-$50,000
       b.  $50,000-$75,000
       c.  $75,000 - $100,000
       d.  $100,000 +

9) Was your income bracket before children based on one or two incomes?

10) What was your job title before you became a mother?

## *History/Family or Origin*

1) Was your mother a Stay-at-Home Mom?

2) What did she call herself?

3) Did she regard motherhood as (state a, b, c, d, or e):

   a. Drudgery
   b. Her life
   c. A sacrifice
   d. A choice
   e. The best years of her life

4) If your mother saw her role as a sacrifice, what was that sacrifice?

## *Career Changes/Challenges*

1) How long were you in your profession before you had children?

2) How did you choose your career?

3) What was your perception of stay-at-home mothers?

4) Prior to having your child, what did you think you would be doing with your career once you had a child? (state a, b, or c):

   a. Keep working full time
   b. Keep working part-time
   c. Quit working all together

5) What did you actually do?

6) What was your impression of how life would change after having children?

7) How has it actually changed, or has it?

8) If you chose not to continue working, outside the home, how do you define yourself? (state a, b, c or d with title):

   a. Housewife
   b. Domestic engineer/CEO of the household
   c. Stay-at-home mom
   d. Other (if so, what title do you use?)

9) Is it a mutual decision for you to stay at home?

10) Do you take your stay-at-home job seriously?

11) Do you perceive your stay-at-home job as a profession?

12) What do you think it would cost someone to pay for outside services to complete everything you do as a mother (e.g. cleaning, raising children, running errands, chauffeuring, daycare)?

13) What is your dollar value for cost/opportunity loss?

14) Do you receive this amount monthly? Yearly?

15) Have you established vacation days for yourself?

16) Have you established sick days for yourself?

17) Do you have the option to not work?

18) What income did you command before children?

19) What salary do you think that you would have reached in the next five years if it were your sole focus?

20) How much does your lifestyle suffer without your income?

21) Does your spouse make enough to compensate for your loss of income?

22) What does your spouse give up by not having your income? What do you give up?

## *Care Taking Issues*

1) When the primary breadwinner cares for the kids, is it considered babysitting?

2) Do you ask the father to watch the kids? Does he offer? Does he suggest and take initiative to have the kids on his own?

3) How satisfying was it to stay at home with one child? (Scale from 1 to 10 with 10 being completely satisfying)

4) How satisfying was it to stay at home with more than one child? (Scale from 1 to 10 with 10 being completely satisfying)

5) Now that you have children, which do you think is more difficult, going to work outside of the home or staying at home with your child/children?

6) Do you feel like you have a support network that you can rely on to help you with the children?

7) Is extended family around that can help you with childcare?

8) Do you feel guilty asking for help?

9) Do you feel that you should be able to do it all yourself?

## *Money Issues*

1) After you were married and/or living with your spouse, were you working in your profession?

2) After you were married and/or living with your spouse, what did you do with the money that you earned?

3) After you were married and/or living with your spouse was the money that you earned "your" money or "our" money?

4) When did you commingle your funds (state a, b, c, d or e):
   a. After moving in together
   b. After marrying
   c. Just before birth of children
   d. After the birth of children
   e. Never commingled

5) Was a joint account set up for running the household prior to having children? After having children?

6) What happened to your earning power since you had a child or children?

7) What happened to your spouse's earning power since you had a child or children?

8) What happened to your spending power once you stopped working in your profession?

9) What happened to your spouse's spending power once you stopped working in your profession?

10) Is the breadwinner's money your money?

11) Was there any discussion about how you would access money for your personal grooming, spending, gift buying, etc?

12) How did you decide and/or who decided how you would access money?

13) Are you on an "allowance" budget?

14) Do you have to ask for money?

15) Do you feel any loss of financial freedom?

16) Do you and your spouse have similar spending habits? If not, who is the spender and who is the saver?

## *Self Image/Self Esteem*

1) Do you have an equal voice since you stopped or downsized your career?

2) Is your job raising the children as important as your partner's career outside the home? (On a scale of 1-10, 10 being as important)

3) Is your life is more stressful or less stressful now that you have children? (On a scale of 1-10, 10 being more stressful)

4) Have you experienced any symptoms of depression since becoming a Mom?

5) Has your social/support system changed in numbers and in actual people?

6) Has your body weight changed? If yes, are you underweight or overweight versus your pre-pregnancy self.

7) Do you and your spouse have dates regularly now that you have children?

8) How often do/did you pamper yourself and how (i.e., massage, pedicure, manicure) pre- and post-motherhood?

9) How often do/did you exercise pre- and post-motherhood?

10) Do you feel that your spouse has more or less respect for you now that you are a Mom?

11) Do you have more or less respect for yourself now that you are a Mom?

# Bibliography

Buchanan, Andrea J. *Mother Shock*, California: Seal Press, 2003

Davis, Kristin. "Can You Afford to Quit Work?" *Parents*, April 2005, pp. 105-109

Fisher, Helen. *The First Sex The Natural Talents of Women and How They are Changing the World*, Random House, 1999

Fox, Faulkner. *Dispatches From a Not-So-Perfect Life*, New York: Harmony Books, 2003

Gore, Ariel. *The Mother Trip*, California: Seal Press, 2000

Halladay, Ayun. *The Big Rumpus*, California: Seal Press, 2002

Hulbert, Ann. "The Real Myth of Motherhood (Reconsidering the Maternal Memoir-Cum Manifesto)." Sandbox, posted Thursday March 8, 2005 at 10:55 am PT.

Kolbe, Kathy. *Pure Instinct, the M.O. of High Performance People and Teams*, Monumentus Press, 2004

Moore, Fernanda. "5 Things I No Longer Feel Guilty About (and Neither Should You)." *Parenting*, June 2005, pp. 99-104

Quindlen, Anna. "The Good Enough Mother." *Newsweek*, February 2004, pp. 50-51

"Study: Stay-at-home Moms Deserve High Pay", *Reuters Limited*, May 2005

Warner, Judith. "Mommy Madness." *Newsweek*, February 2005, pp. 42-49

Printed in the United States
143616LV00007B/84/A